Alexander P. Saccaro, Alois Mayer, Philip Hewitt

Das große Trainingsbuch

Englisch

5. + 6. Schuljahr

- Der komplette Lernstoff
- Grammatik
- Rechtschreibung
- Diktate
- Viele Übungen mit Lösungen

Ernst Klett Verlag
Stuttgart Düsseldorf Leipzig

Die Deutsche Bibliothek – CIP-Einheitsaufnahmen

Der Titelsatz für diese Publikation ist bei Der Deutschen Bibliothek erhältlich

Autoren

Philip Hewitt:
Seiten 160 – 164; 166 – 208; 214; 219 – 223; 233 – 238; 241; 293 – 302

Alois Mayer:
Seiten 142 – 159; 165; 211 – 213; 215 – 218; 224 – 230; 239 – 240; 287 – 292

Alexander P. Saccaro:
Seiten 9 – 138; 245 – 286

Auflage 4. 3. 2. | 2005 2004 2003
Die letzten Zahlen bezeichnen jeweils die Auflage und das Jahr des Druckes

Internetadresse: http://www.klett-lerntraining.de
E-Mail: klett-kundenservice@klett-mail.de
Umschlaggestaltung: Bayerl und Ost, Frankfurt/M.
Zeichnungen: Andreas Florian, Lübeck
DTP: Klaus Bauer, Bondorf
Druck: Konradin Druck GmbH, 70771 Leinfelden-Echterdingen
Printed in Germany
ISBN: 3-12-922040-2

GRAMMATIK

RECHTSCHREIBUNG

DIKTATE

LÖSUNGEN

GRAMMATIK

Liebe Schülerin, lieber Schüler,

es ist eine alte Tatsache: Wer lernt, macht Fehler. Doch sollte man bestimmte Fehler nicht immer wieder machen, zumal sie sich leicht vermeiden lassen, wenn man etwas aufpasst. Dazu möchte der Grammatikteil dieses Buches beitragen: Er soll dir helfen, typische Fehler zu vermeiden.

Dazu musst du allerdings auch selbst etwas tun, denn ganz ohne Lernen geht die Sache nicht. Wenn du nicht bereit bist, z. B. die Formen von *to be* so zu lernen, dass du sie auch im Schlaf aufsagen kannst, wird dir auch ein noch so großes Verständnis für die englische Grammatik nur wenig nutzen. Bei einer Sprache muss man zwar vieles auch verstehen, aber fast wichtiger noch ist das einwandfreie Beherrschen der Grundformen.

Der Grammatikteil umfasst den wesentlichen Stoff der ersten beiden Lernjahre. Er ist in 20 Kapitel eingeteilt, die du unabhängig voneinander durchnehmen kannst. Die Anordnung der einzelnen Kapitel lehnt sich an die Durchnahme des Grammatikstoffes in der Schule an, so dass du dieses Buch schon früh benutzen kannst – zum Teil sogar parallel zum Unterricht. Die Übungen sind nach ihrem Schwierigkeitsgrad angeordnet und auf typische Fehler abgestimmt.

Du kannst diesen Teil Kapitel für Kapitel durcharbeiten und so deine Grammatikkenntnisse rundherum auffrischen. Oder du übst gezielt nur den Stoff einzelner Kapitel – als Vorbereitung auf eine Klassenarbeit zum Beispiel oder um einzelne Lücken zu schließen. Das Ergebnis deiner Anstrengungen kannst du danach – bitte nicht vorher! – mit den Lösungen vergleichen.

Zu vielen Kapiteln des Teils „Grammatik“ gibt es passende Diktate. Mit ihnen kannst du Rechtschreibregeln üben, die mit den Grammatikthemen zusammenhängen – zum Beispiel Besonderheiten in der Schreibung vor der Endung *-s* im *simple present* oder vor der Endung *-ed* im *simple past.*

Substantive

1

Weißt du noch, was Substantive bzw. Nomen sind? Grob gesagt, sind es Wörter, mit denen wir Personen, Tiere, Sachen, Gegenstände und abstrakte Begriffe wie Eigenschaften und Gefühle bezeichnen. Viele dieser Substantive können auch im Plural gebraucht werden.

REGEL

Die regelmäßige Bildung des Plurals

Im Allgemeinen bildet man den Plural im Englischen, indem man an die Singularform ein **-s** (nach Zischlauten ein **-es,** wenn kein **-e** vorhanden ist) anhängt:

Singular	Plural	Singular	Plural
a farm	farms	a bus	buses
a hen	hens	a sponge	sponges

Aufgepasst:

- auslautendes **-y** wird nach Konsonant zu **-ies:**
  a baby — babies
- auslautendes **-fe** wird meist zu **-ves:**
  a knife — knives

Unregelmäßige Pluralformen

a man	two men	a foot	two feet
a woman	three women	a goose	ten geese
a child	five children	a mouse	three mice

ÜBUNG 1 Mr Mason's farm

Mr Mason is Tom's grandad. He has got a farm near York. Look at the picture of his farm.

a) What people and animals are there on the farm?
b) Make a list of all the nouns. Put the singular nouns in the plural and the plural nouns in the singular.

Example: a farmhouse — farmhouses
a wife — ____________

ÜBUNG 2 Animals, animals

There are other animals on a farm, too.

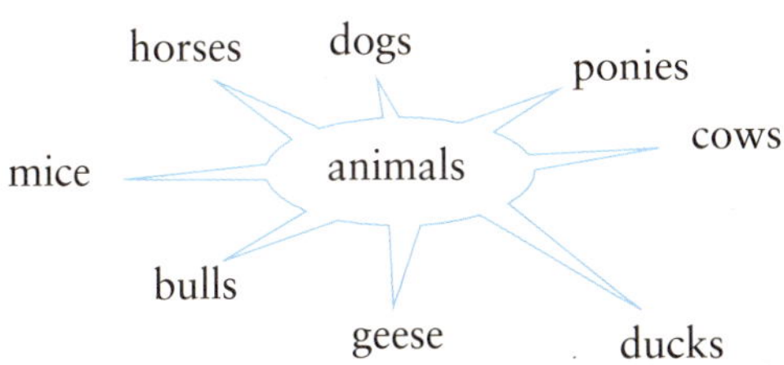

What is the singular of these nouns?

ÜBUNG 3 **Mr Mason's birthday**

Fill in the right nouns.

There are a lot of  ______,  ______ and  ______ on Mr Mason's farm today. They have all got  ______ for Mr Mason because it is his birthday. Look at those two  ______ over there; the big boy is Tom and the small boy is Timmy. They have got presents, too. Tom's present is a book about farm animals. Timmy has got something in his  ______, too. But it is not a  ______, it is only his old  ______. Poor teddy! One  ______ is missing and one  ______, too, and it is half-blind because one  ______ is gone. Timmy has got a present for his grandad, too. It is a wonderful picture of three big  ______. They are in the kitchen and they are eating grandpa's birthday  ______.

ACHTUNG

Look at that man over there! That's Tom's grandad, Mr Mason. He is a farmer, but today he is not wearing his old trousers, his old shirt and his old shoes. He has got his best clothes on because it is his birthday. Mrs Mason is wearing her best clothes, too. She is not wearing her old jeans, but a nice blouse, a new skirt and some nice tights.

Clothes, jeans, trousers und *tights* (= Strumpfhosen) werden im Englischen immer im Plural gebraucht.
Der unbestimmte Artikel *a/an* ist vor diesen Substantiven nicht möglich.

ÜBUNG 4 Kate's clothes

Look at this girl. It's Kate, Tom's sister. Well, it's grandpa's birthday, but she has got all her old clothes on.

Complete the sentences.

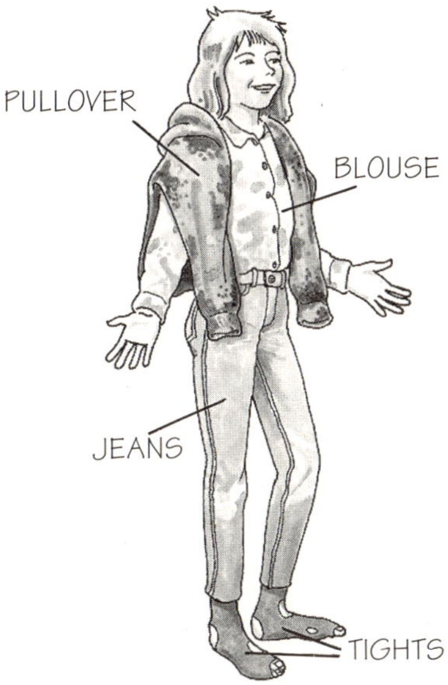

Look at her old pullover.

It is dirty.

Look at her old tights.

There ____________ holes in ____________ .

Look at her old jeans.

____________ too small.

Look at her old blouse.

____________ not clean.

Her clothes ____________ really awful!

ÜBUNG 5 **Your clothes**

a) What are you wearing now?

b) What clothes do you like best?

ACHTUNG

Auch *police* und *people* (= Leute) werden im Englischen immer wie Pluralwörter gebraucht.
Homework steht dagegen im Englischen immer im Singular.

Help! Where are the police?
Some people give us too much homework!

DIKTAT 1

Und jetzt solltest du als Abschluss dieses Kapitels ein kurzes Diktat schreiben. Lass dir den Text diktieren: Diktat Nr. 1.
In dem Diktat kommen zwei Wörter vor, die du vielleicht noch nicht kennst:

to shake [ʃeɪk] – hier: schütten
shiny [ˈʃaɪnɪ] – glänzend

Präge dir die Wörter gut ein.

2 Das Personalpronomen

REGEL

Das Personalpronomen als Subjekt

Where is Kate?	She	is here.
Where is Tom?	He	is at school.
Where is your book?	It	isn't here.
	Subjekt	

Pronomen stehen immer für (= pro) ein Substantiv (= Nomen). Ist das Pronomen das Subjekt eines Satzes, so lauten seine Formen:

I	you	he	she	it	we	you	they
(ich)	(du/Sie)	(er)	(sie)	(es)	(wir)	(ihr/Sie)	(sie)
	Singular					**Plural**	

It steht für Sachen; *they* kann für Sachen und Personen stehen. Alle anderen Personalpronomen stehen für Personen.

ÜBUNG 1 **Where are they?**

Answer these questions. Use pronouns in your answers.

1. Where is Mr Mason? — (on the farm)

2. Where is Mrs Mason? — (in the house)

3. Where is Tom? — (at school)

4. Where is Tom's bike?

(at school, too)

5. Where is Timmy?

(on his potty)

(on the floor)

6. Where are his toys?

7. Where are his clothes?

(on his bed)

8. Where is Kate?

(not at home)

(with her)

9. Where is her girlfriend?

10. Where are Kate and Jenny?

(in the park)

ÜBUNG 2 **At school**

Teachers ask a lot of questions. Ask and answer them.

Where is Where are	Tom and Mike? your homework? your English book? your book? Christine? the register? they from? you from? Kate?	in the classroom here on the bus on the desk at home not here in my schoolbag ill York at school

REGEL

Das Personalpronomen als Objekt

Personalpronomen können auch Objekt eines Satzes sein. Ihre Formen lauten dann:

		me	(mir/mich)
		you	(dir/dich/Ihnen)
Tom	can help	him	(ihm/ihn)
Kate	can see	her	(ihr/sie)
		it	(ihm/es)
		us	(uns)
		you	(euch/Ihnen)
		them	(ihnen/sie)
		Objekt	

Im Englischen macht man bei den Pronomen keinen Unterschied zwischen dem indirekten und direkten Objekt; die Formen sind gleich. Wie bei den Subjektpronomen steht *it* für eine Sache; *them* kann für Sachen und Personen stehen.

Die Objektform des Personalpronomens steht im Englischen auch nach Präpositionen:

Wait for me! Look at her!
Look at him! Wait for them!

ÜBUNG 3

Looking for things and persons

Answer the questions. Use pronouns.

1. Where are my clothes?
2. Where is my book?
3. Where are you, Kate?
4. Where is Mike?
5. Where are Tom and Jenny?
6. Where are my photos?
7. Where are my keys?
8. Where is my money?
9. Where is Dad?
10. Where is your potty, Timmy?
11. Where is my teddy?
12. Where are my trousers?

I can't find ________. I can't see ________. I can't hear ________.

ÜBUNG **4** **Asking Timmy**

Fill in the missing pronouns.

Kate: Where are you, Timmy?

I can't see ________ .

Timmy: ________ 'm here.

Kate: Where is your potty?

Timmy: ________ 's not here.

I can't find ________ .

Kate: Where is your teddy?

Timmy: ________ 's in my bed. I see ________ from here.

Kate: Where are your trousers?

I can't see ________ .

Timmy: I really don't know.

Kate: Come on, Timmy, where are ________ ?

Timmy (crying): ________ are in my room.

Kate: Why are ________ crying, Timmy?

Timmy (still crying): I don't like these trousers. ________ are bad trousers.

Kate: Why, Timmy? Are ________ wet again?

Timmy (still crying): Yes, ________ are.

Kate: Don't cry, Timmy. Let's wash ________ . Help ________ .

ÜBUNG 5 Looking for Timmy's trousers

Kate is upstairs in Timmy's room. She is looking for his trousers, but she can't find them. Complete the sentences.

Kate: Timmy, where are ________?

Help ________ to look for ________ .

Are ________ under your bed?

Timmy: No, ________ aren't. ________ aren't there.

Kate: Where are ________ then? Let ________ guess.

Are ________ in your bed?

Timmy: No, ________ aren't in my bed. ________ are in my teddy's bed.

Kate: In your teddy's bed? Where is ________?

Timmy: ________'s here.

Kate: But why are ________ in your teddy's bed, Timmy?

Timmy: It's my teddy who makes ________ wet, not me.

Kate: Then call your teddy and tell ________ to help ________ .

3

Der bestimmte und der unbestimmte Artikel

REGEL

Der unbestimmte Artikel

a) Formen

a [ə]	an [ən]
a book	an apple
a yellow car	an empty car
a nice uncle	an uncle
a uniform	an old uniform

Der unbestimmte Artikel hat im Englischen zwei Formen: *a* und *an*. Vor einem folgenden Vokal steht *an*, vor einem folgenden Konsonant *a*. Vor dem Halbvokal [j] (wie in *unit, uniform, yellow)* steht *a*.

ÜBUNG 1 **Tom's schoolbag**

Do you pack your schoolbag every day? Well, Tom doesn't. There are a lot of things in Tom's schoolbag:

________ empty bottle
________ German book
________ apple
________ English book
________ old sandwich
________ pencil-case
________ exercise book
________ workbook
________ water-pistol

REGEL

b) Zum Gebrauch des unbestimmten Artikels

Tom has got a new girlfriend.
Her father is a taxi-driver.
She's ill today; she's got a headache and a temperature.

Der unbestimmte Artikel bezeichnet einzelne Dinge oder Personen. Im Unterschied zum Deutschen steht er bei Berufsbezeichnungen und bei bestimmten Ausdrücken wie *to have (got) a headache/a temperature* (= Kopfweh, Fieber haben).

ÜBUNG 2

Who are they?

Example: 1. He is a milkman.

1. He brings the milk in the morning.

2. He brings you letters and parcels.

3. You go to him when you want to buy sausages.

4. He sells you all kind of vegetables.

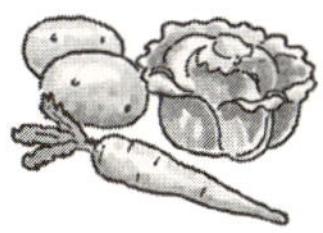

5. She helps you to find what you want when you are in a shop.

6. She works for a newspaper.

7. He comes when your house is on fire.

8. He helps animals when they are ill.

REGEL

Der bestimmte Artikel

a) Die Aussprache des bestimmten Artikels

the boy	the other girl
the car	the English car
the uniform	the old uniform
the yellow book	the easy unit
[ðə]	[ðɪ]

Es gibt im Englischen nur eine Form des bestimmten Artikels. Seine Aussprache richtet sich nach dem folgenden Wort. Vor einem Vokal wird *the* [ðɪ], vor einem Konsonant und [j] wird er [ðə] ausgesprochen.

ÜBUNG 3

What's right?

Say the words with [ðə] or [ðɪ]. *Example:* [ðə] box, [ðɪ] empty box.

_____ old women	_____ young girls	_____ American cars
_____ English children	_____ silly answer	_____ difficult question
_____ example	_____ bad ideas	_____ school uniforms
_____ yellow apples	_____ afternoons .	_____ empty pages

REGEL

b) Zum Gebrauch des bestimmten Artikels

1. The colours of Tom's school uniform are blue and grey. The girls must wear a grey skirt and the boys must wear grey trousers.	1. Der bestimmte Artikel steht immer, wenn es sich um bestimmte Personen oder Sachen handelt.
2. Not all boys and girls in Britain like school uniforms.	2. Wenn diese nicht näher bestimmt sind, steht der bestimmte Artikel nicht.
3. Tom goes to school by bus. Some children go there by train.	3. Der bestimmte Artikel steht auch nicht bei Eigennamen im Singular und bei Verkehrsmitteln, wenn man sagen will, wie man irgendwo hinkommt.

ACHTUNG

Bei Wörtern wie *bed* und *school* steht kein Artikel, wenn man ausdrücken will, was man dort tut. Ist dagegen das Möbelstück oder das Gebäude gemeint, so steht der bestimmte Artikel:

Let's go to bed.
= Gehen wir ins Bett (= schlafen).

Let's look under the bed.
= Schauen wir unter dem Bett nach.

He goes to school.
= Er geht zur Schule (= in den Unterricht).

His mother is going to the school.
= Seine Mutter geht in die Schule.

ÜBUNG 4 Definite article or not?

Complete the sentences.

1. ______ boys like ______ girls.
2. ______ Tom likes ______ Jenny.
3. Do you like ______ boys in your class?
4. Do you usually like ______ girls more than ______ boys?
5. What about ______ girls in your class? Are they nice?
6. Which of ______ boys/girls do you like best?
7. Who is ______ nicest boy/girl in your class?
8. What's ______ name of the girl/boy you like best?
9. Are ______ girls/boys in your class good at English?
10. Are ______ boys as clever as ______ girls? What do you think?

ÜBUNG 5 **Jenny**

Definite article or not? Complete the sentences.

Jenny is not Tom's sister, she is ______ Tom's friend. She lives in ______ Apple Street. ______ Apple Street is a small street in ______ north of ______ York. In winter she goes to ______ school by ______ bus, in summer she goes to ______ school by ______ bike. ______ Tom is in her class. She doesn't like all ______ girls and boys in her class, but she likes ______ Tom very much. She thinks he is ______ nicest boy in her class. But Jenny doesn't only like ______ Tom, she also likes ______ maths. ______ maths is ______ subject she likes best. Before ______ tests, she always helps ______ Tom. Jenny also likes ______ pets. She hasn't got a pet yet, but she can have a pet for her birthday.

ÜBUNG 6 **Jenny is ill**

Where is a definite or indefinite article missing?

Jenny goes to ______ same school as ______ Tom. Sometimes Tom's father takes them to ______ school in ______ morning. ______ school they go to is ______ big school. There are a lot of ______ pupils at Jenny's school, and not all of them like ______ school. But Jenny does; she likes ______ school because most of ______ teachers she has got are really good. Today she can't go to ______ school; she must stay in ______ bed, but she hasn't got ______ temperature. She's got ______ cold and ______ bad headache. She feels terrible and she doesn't want to eat anything. She just wants to see ______ doctor and stay in ______ bed. Poor Jenny!

ÜBUNG 7 **How can you get there?**

Today there is a geography lesson. The children are talking about how they can get to other towns or countries. Be careful! Tom and the other children live in York.

Example: What about London? How can you get there?
I can get there by train.

Germany
Scotland
Ireland
Denmark
France
The Isle of Wight
Wales

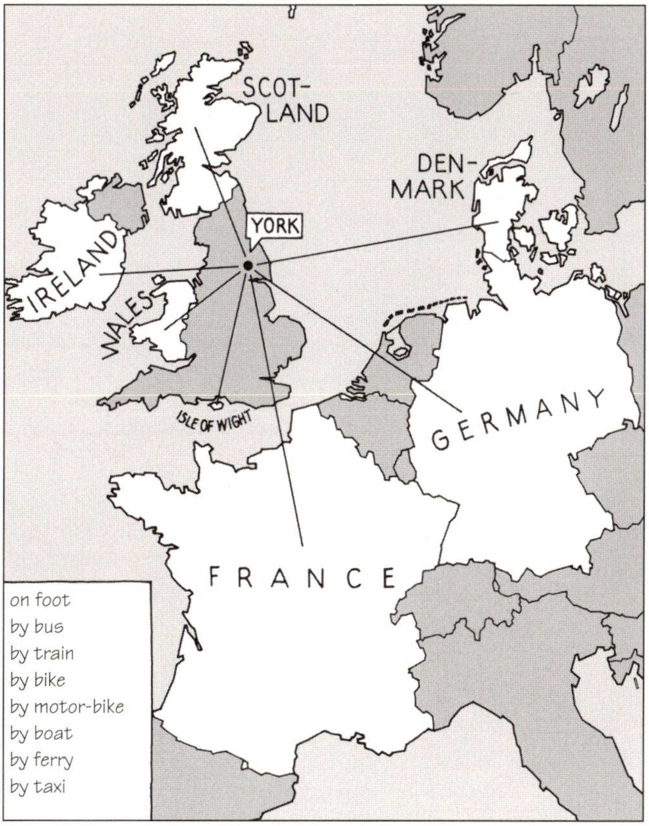

ferry – Fähre

4 Substantive und ihre Begleiter

Englische wie deutsche Substantive stehen nicht immer allein. Sie werden häufig von anderen Wörtern „begleitet", die sie näher bestimmen. In der deutschen Grammatik nennt man diese Wörter daher „Begleiter"; in der englischen Grammatik heißen sie *determiners*. Zu diesen Begleitern gehören unter anderem:

REGEL

Die Possessivbegleiter

Formen:

This isn't	my	book.
Is it	your	book?
No, it isn't. It's	her	book.
No, it's	his	book.
Oh, no. Is it	your	book, Tom and Kevin?
Let's see. No, it isn't	our	book. Perhaps it's the girls' book.
Yes, it is. It's	their	book.

My, your etc. drücken Besitz oder Zugehörigkeit aus. Mit Ausnahme von *their*, das sich auch auf Sachen beziehen kann, beziehen sich *my, your* usw. immer auf Personen. Dabei kann *your* verschiedene Bedeutungen haben:

Is that your mother, Tom?	(deine Mutter)
Is that your son, Mrs Mason?	(Ihr Sohn)
Is that your bike, Jenny and Kate?	(euer Fahrrad)

Neben diesen Formen kommt auch *its* vor. *Its* bezieht sich immer auf eine Sache:
This is our school. Its classrooms are very nice.
This is Tom's bike. Its saddle is new.

ÜBUNG 1 Everybody has got something

Add the possessive determiners.
Example: Timmy has got a teddy. It's his teddy.

1. Tom's grandparents have got a farm. It's ________
2. The Masons have got a flat. ________
3. Mr and Mrs Mason have got a car. ________
4. Tom has got a sister. ________
5. Kate has got a brother. ________
6. Timmy has got a lot of toys. ________
7. Mike has got a camera. ________
8. Jenny has got a boyfriend. ________

ÜBUNG 2 Timmy's "toys"

Baby brothers and baby sisters often "find" things that belong to other people. Timmy does, too. He has got a big collection of things.

Complete what Mum says:

1. What have you got here, Timmy? Let me see – an exercise book. Look, Timmy, it's not ________ exercise-book, it's Kate's. It's ________ exercise-book.

2. Where have you got that from, Timmy? Kate's German book! How can Kate do German tests when you keep it under ________ bed? What will ________ teacher say?

3. What about these keys, Timmy? Aren't they Dad's keys? I think they are ________ keys.

4. And look, Timmy. This is not ________ picture book, it's Kate's. It was ________ birthday present from Tom. So you can't keep it.

5. Don't cry, Timmy. Look, you've got so many things: here's ________ teddy, here's ________ van, here's ________ telephone. So play with ________ things now.

ACHTUNG

Verwechsle nicht *you* mit *your, its* mit *it's, they* mit *their* und *they're* mit *there!*

Timmy, where are you?
Where is your teddy?

It's Tom's bike. Its saddle is new. It's got a new bell, too.

Are Tom and Mike there? No, they aren't. They're at school.

Where are their bikes?
They're over there.

1. *your, its, their* sind Possessivbegleiter. Sie stehen immer vor einem Substantiv.
2. *they* ist ein Pronomen und steht für ein Substantiv im Plural. *They're* ist die Kurzform von *they are.*
3. *there* (= da, dort/dahin, dorthin) steht entweder allein oder vor einer Form von *to be* (= es gibt).

Nach *there is* muss das Substantiv im Singular stehen; nach *there are* folgt ein Substantiv im Plural:
There is a boy over there and there are some girls there, too.

ÜBUNG 3 **Your room**

Put in "you" or "your", then answer the questions.

1. What about _______ room? Do _______ like it?
2. Do _______ clean it or does _______ mother clean it?
3. What's in _______ room?
4. Is there anything under _______ bed?
5. Where do _______ keep _______ clothes?
6. Where do _______ do _______ homework?
7. Have _______ got a TV in _______ room?
8. Have _______ got posters and photos in _______ room, too?

ÜBUNG 4

Tom's room.

Put in "its", "it's", "they", "their" or "there".

_______ are a lot of things in Tom's room. _______ are books and cassettes everywhere. _______ are on the chairs, on his bed and on the floor. And _______ is something under his bed. What is it? _______ an old pullover. _______ are some socks under his bed, too. _______ are holes in them and _______ look dirty. And what's that on the wall? _______ are a lot of photos and posters on the wall over his bed. Look at that photo over_______. _______ a photo of Jenny. She is sitting on her bike. _______ not a new bike, but _______ handlebars and _______ saddle are new.

REGEL

Die Demonstrativbegleiter

Look at this book. This isn't my book.

And what about that book over there?

Yes, it is. And what about these pencils? Aren't they your pencils?

No, they aren't. But give me those pencils over there. They may be my pencils.

This/these verweisen auf Dinge oder Personen, die in der Nähe des Sprechers sind; *that/those* verweisen dagegen auf Dinge oder Personen, die weiter entfernt sind.

Aufgepasst:
Ob du *this/that* oder *these/those* gebrauchen musst, hängt von dem nachfolgenden Substantiv ab. Steht das Substantiv im Singular, steht immer *this/that*; steht das Substantiv im Plural, steht immer *these/those*.

This is my book and that is your book.
These are my pencils and those are your pencils.

ÜBUNG 5 **Timmy at school**

Today Mrs Mason must see a doctor and Mr Mason can't stay at home, so Tom takes Timmy to school. Timmy wants to know everything.
Put in "this" or "that".

Timmy: Is ______ your classroom, Tom?

Tom: No Timmy, ______ isn't my classroom. My classroom is over there.

Timmy: Is ______ your class, Tom?

Tom: Yes, ______ is my class.

Timmy: And ______ class over there?

Tom: ______'s Kate's class.

Timmy: Is ______ your chair here?

Tom: Yes, it is. And look, Timmy, ______ chair over there, ______'s Jenny's.

Timmy: What's the name of ______ fat boy over there, Tommy?

Tom: His name is John, but don't call him fat because he doesn't like it.

Timmy: Is ______ a teacher over there, Tom?

Tom: No, it isn't. It's a pupil, Timmy.

Timmy: But ______ is a teacher, Tom.

Tom: Where? Over there? Ah yes, ______'s our English teacher. You're right, Timmy.

Timmy: And the girl beside him is his daughter?

Tom: No, Timmy, it isn't. It's a girl in Kate's class.

ÜBUNG 6 **No, Timmy ...**

Timmy has collected a lot of things again, but Kate and Tom don't let him have everything.

Example: No, Timmy, this isn't your picture book. It's Kate's.
Look! Your picture book is over there.

Go on. Use the following nouns:

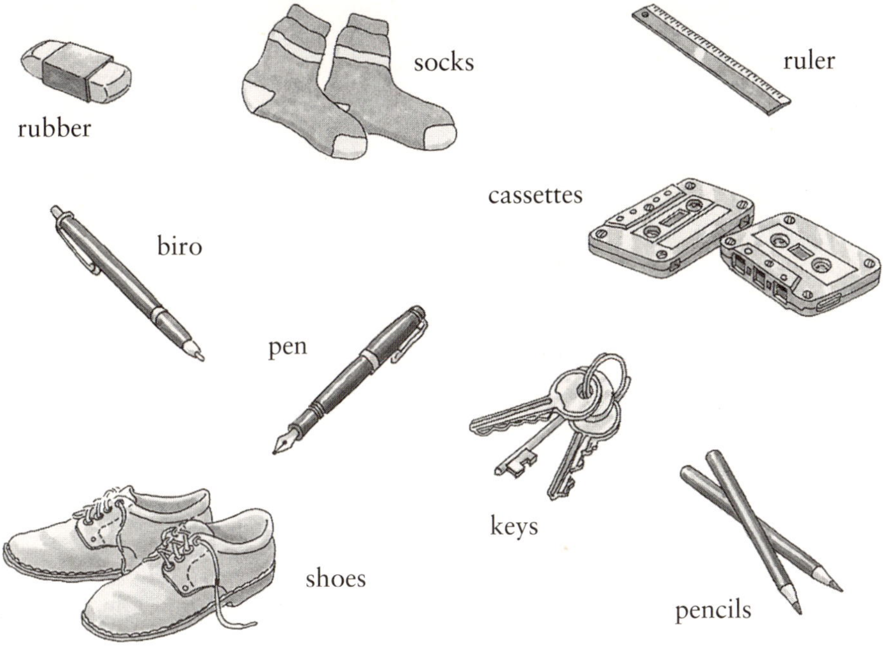

REGEL

Much und many

Zu den Begleitern zählen auch *much* und *many*. Beide entsprechen, wenn sie vor einem Substantiv stehen, dem Deutschen „viel(e)“.

What about your class? Are there many girls in it? How many teachers have you got?

Many kann nur bei einem Substantiv im Plural stehen.

How much homework do you get? Is it too much or just right? How much time do you spend on your homework?

Much steht nur bei einem Substantiv im Singular.

Do you like English very much?

Bezieht sich *much* auf ein Verb, so bedeutet es meistens „sehr“.

ÜBUNG 7 **A questionnaire**

Put in "much" or "many".

1. How ________ homework have you got today?
2. How ________ time do you usually spend on it?
3. How ________ minutes do you spend on your English homework?
4. How ________ hours do you spend in front of the TV?
5. How ________ subjects have you got?
6. How ________ help do you get from your parents?
7. How ________ tests do you have a year?
8. How ________ good marks did you get last year?
9. How ________ tests have you written this week?
10. How ________ money do you get for good marks?

ÜBUNG 8 **What's school?**

Complete with "much" or "many".

Well, school is

too ____________ tests.

too ____________ bad marks.

too ____________ questions.

too ____________ teachers.

too ____________ boring subjects.

too ____________ homework.

too ____________ time indoors.

too ________ work.

That's why I love school so ____________.

Der s- und der of-Genitiv

5

REGEL

Der s-Genitiv

Der *s*-Genitiv steht im Englischen zumeist bei Personen. Wie *my, your* etc. gibt er an, wem etwas gehört oder wem etwas zuzuordnen ist. Seine Formen sind:

<u>Singular:</u> ... 's
Kate's book
a child's voice

<u>Regelmäßiger Plural:</u> ... s'
the girls' books
my parents' house

<u>Unregelmäßiger Plural:</u> ... 's
children's voices
people's ideas

ACHTUNG

Verwechsle den *s*-Genitiv nicht mit dem Plural -*s*. Beim Plural steht nie ein Apostroph!
My parents are not at home.

Auch bei der 3. Person Einzahl im *simple present* steht nie ein Apostroph.
He works in an office.

Verwechsle den s-Genitiv auch nicht mit den Kurzformen von *is* und *has ('s)*.

ÜBUNG 1

The s-genitive

Write out the s-genitive forms.

Timmy/toys

Timmy's toys

the boys/teacher

the girls/schoolbags

our cat/food

Kate/friends

women/clothes

the man/boots

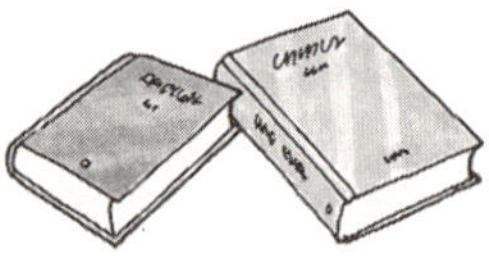

the children/books

girls/school uniforms

Jenny/dog

the Masons/house

my parents/car

ÜBUNG 2 A dialogue

Ask the questions and answer them.

Is this your / Are these your	toys, Tom?	No,	(baby brother)
	girlfriend, Kevin?	No,	(Tom)
	magazine, Jenny?	No,	(the girls)
	cat, Kate?	No,	(my mother)
	homework, Joe?	No, they aren't. They are …	(Kevin)
	house, Mr Mason?	No, it isn't. It's …	(grandparents)
	bike, Kate?	No,	(Jenny)
	room, Tom?	No,	(my sister)
	teddy, Jenny?	No,	(Timmy)
	van, Timmy?	Yes, it is. It's my van!	

ÜBUNG 3 Timmy's treasures

Put in the missing -s and the apostrophes.

Timmy is Tom___ baby brother. He is three years old. One of his favourite toy___ is his teddy; but he___ got other toy___ , too. He keeps them in his cupboard; but there are other thing___ in his cupboard. Look! There___ one of Jenny___ letter___ to Tom; there___ an old German book and there___ Kate___ ruler. There are also some key___ ; are they his parent___ key___? There___ a tennis ball, too. Whose is it? Is it Kevin___or Joe___? It can't be Kate___ or Tom___ because they don't play tennis.

ÜBUNG 4 Jenny

The s-genitive or a short form? Mark with different colours.

Jenny is Tom's girlfriend. She's twelve. She hasn't got a brother or a sister; she's only got her parents. Jenny is from York; her mother is from York, too, but her father is from Nottingham. They live in an old house; it's her grandparents' house. Jenny's other relatives live in London; she's got an aunt there who's over sixty and who's got a flat in London. She hasn't got any children, so Jenny is her only niece. In her summer holidays Jenny wants to see her: it will be Jenny's first visit to London.

REGEL

Der *of*-Genitiv

Der *of*-Genitiv (oft auch *of-phrase* genannt) drückt Zugehörigkeit und Mengenangaben aus. Im Unterschied zum *s*-Genitiv steht er meist nur bei Sachen.

the pages of a book the legs of the table	a bottle of lemonade a pound of apples
Zugehörigkeit	**Mengenangaben**

ÜBUNG 5 **The of- or the s-genitive?**

Example: the boys' legs – the doors of my room

the boys/legs	the girl/hands	the car/windows
the doors/my room	the dog/feet	my neighbour/cat
Kate/books	the children/clothes	the end/school
on the evening/my birthday	the light/the moon	Jenny/story

ÜBUNG 6 **What goes together?**

Example: a bar of chocolate

a bar	of	milk	a tin	of	cornflakes
lots	of	tea	a pound	of	crisps
a glass	of	food	a bag	of	cheese
a cup	of	strawberries	a packet	of	peas
a plate	of	chocolate	a piece	of	sausages

ÜBUNG 7 Tom's shopping list

In a few days it's Tom's birthday. He wants to invite some friends and have a party. The day before the party he goes with his friend Mike to Mrs White's corner shop to buy some things. Here is his shopping list. Can you complete it?

five ______________ crisps

three ______________ biscuits

five ______________ coke

five ______________ lemonade

three ______________ sausages

two ______________ pineapples

five ______________ ice cream

ACHTUNG

Verwechslungsmöglichkeiten

Tom takes some money out of his purse.
The purse falls off the table.
Hands off! It's Tom's purse.

Sei vorsichtig. Der *of*-Genitiv wird oft mit der Präposition *off* (von … herunter/weg) oder mit *out of* (aus/heraus) verwechselt.

I've got a postcard from my father. It's from London. There are greetings from all the family on it.

Verwechsle den *of*- und den *s*-Genitiv nicht mit der Präposition *from*. Die Präposition *from* gibt meist eine Richtung von einer Person oder von einem Ort her an.

ÜBUNG 8 **The s-genitive, of, out of, off or from?**

Complete the text.

"Get ______ that bike," Tom said to Mike, "Let's put all the things on it. Then we needn't carry them." So they put all their things on Tom ______ bike. "Be careful, Mike, hold the bottles or they will fall ______ the bike." So Mike took one hand ______ his pockets and tried to hold them. It was not very far ______ the corner shop to the Masons ______ flat – only a five minutes' walk. But soon there was a loud crash and the bottles fell ______ the bike. Two bottles ______ lemonade were broken. So they had to go back to Mrs White ______ shop. This time they got home all right. No bottles fell ______ the bike and Mike even took both hands ______ his pockets.

At home, they carried everything into the kitchen. Then they went upstairs into Tom ______ room and talked about the party. Five minutes later there was a telephone call ______ Jenny ______ mother. "Jenny is ill, Tom. She's just come home ______ school and she looks really ill. I'm afraid she can't come to your party. But I nearly forgot to wish you all the best for your birthday – greetings ______ Jenny and ______ my husband. You will hear ______ Jenny tomorrow. Bye, Tom, and have a nice party!"

DIKTATE 2 3 4

Zu diesem schwierigen Kapitel kannst du drei Diktate schreiben: Nr. 2, 3 und 4.

6 Das Präsens von „haben“

REGEL

Formen

Bejahte Formen		Verneinte Formen	
Langformen	Kurzformen	Langformen	Kurzformen
I have got	I've got	I have not got	I haven't got
you have got	you've got	you have not got	you haven't got
he has got	he's got	he has not got	he hasn't got
she has got	she's got	she has not got	she hasn't got
it has got	it's got	it has not got	it hasn't got
we have got	we've got	we have not got	we haven't got
you have got	you've got	you have not got	you haven't got
they have got	they've got	they have not got	they haven't got

Bei *haven't* fällt das **-e** nicht aus. Der Apostroph steht nur für ein ausgefallenes **-o**. Bei has steht nie ein **-e**.

Ob du *have got* oder *has got* gebrauchen musst, hängt vom Subjekt ab:

Kate	has got	a bike.
My friends	have got	bikes, too.

ÜBUNG 1

The Masons' house

Put in the correct forms of "have got".

1. Tom's parents live in York. They ______________ a flat there.
2. They ______________ five rooms.
3. Tom ______________ a room, and Kate ______________ a room , too.
4. Timmy ______________ a big room. His room is small.
5. The Masons ______________ a car.
6. Tom and Kate ______________ a car, they ______________ bikes.
7. Timmy ______________ a bike because he's too young.
8. But he ______________ two big toy cars and other toys in his room.

ÜBUNG 2

Timmy's toys

Timmy has got a cat, a dog, a teddy, two buckets, a telephone, some toy cars and two or three picture books.

a) Now you are Timmy. Tell your friends what you have got.
b) What about you? What have you got?

ÜBUNG 3

What Kate has got

a) *Example:* Kate has got two brothers, but she hasn't got a sister.

two brothers

boyfriend

bike

sister

a lot of friends

car

a teddy

a football

a radio

toy car

dog

TV

b) What about you? – I have got ... , but I haven't got ...

c) What about your friend(s)? Have they got brothers, sisters, etc.?

REGEL

Fragen und Kurzantworten

Has	Kate	got	a brother?	Yes,	she	has.
Has	Kate	got	a sister?	No,	she	hasn't.
Have	her parents	got	a house?	No,	they	haven't.
Have	they	got	a flat?	Yes,	they	have.
has/have	**Subjekt**	***got***			**Subjekt (Pronomen)**	Form von *have*

Bei Fragen stehen *have/has* vor dem Subjekt. *Got* steht nach dem Subjekt.

Bei Kurzantworten musst du das Subjekt als Pronomen wiederholen.
Nach *yes* steht eine bejahte Langform, nach *no* eine verneinte Kurzform. *Got* entfällt.

ÜBUNG 4 **Kate**

a) Look at exercise 3, then ask questions and give short answers.

1. Has Kate got a brother? Yes, she …
2. Has she got a sister? No, she …

Go on.

b) Ask Kate.

Have you got a brother, Kate? Yes, I …

Go on.

ÜBUNG 5 **What about you?**

Ask as many questions as you can and give short answers.

	you		a car	
	your parents		a lot of toys	
	your friends		a house	
Has	your mother	got	a water-pistol	Yes, …
Have	your grandmother		an English book	No, …
	your English teacher		a toy car	
	your boyfriend		a potty	
	your father		a hamster	

Das Präsens von „sein“

7

REGEL

Formen

Bejahte Formen		Verneinte Formen	
Langformen	Kurzformen	Langformen	Kurzformen
I am	I'm	I am not	I'm not
you are	you're	you are not	you aren't
he is	he's	he is not	he isn't
she is	she's	she is not	she isn't
it is	it's	it is not	it isn't
we are	we're	we are not	we aren't
you are	you're	you are not	you aren't
they are	they're	they are not	they aren't

Der Apostroph in den Kurzformen steht auch hier für einen ausgefallenen Vokal, z.B. für das *o* in *isn't/aren't.*

Auch bei *to be* richtet sich die Form des Verbs nach dem Subjekt:

I	am	ill.
They	are	my friends.

ÜBUNG 1 **Tom's birthday**

Put in the right forms of "to be".

Today, it ______ Tom's birthday. He ______ twelve years old today. All his friends ______ there. His sister ______ there, too. Her name ______ Kate. She ______ eleven years old. Only Jenny, his girlfriend, ______ not there. Where ______ she? She ______ ill. They ______ all in the kitchen; it ______ full of children. They ______ all hungry and thirsty. There ______ a lot of sandwiches on the table; there ______ some bottles of lemonade, too. But one bottle ______ on the floor; it ______ broken and there ______ a pool of lemonade around it. And who ______ in the pool? It ______ Timmy, Tom's baby brother.

ÜBUNG 2 **Tom's friends**

Tom tells us everything about his friends and his family.
Complete the sentences with forms of "to be".

That ______ Kevin and that ______ Joe.
They ______ my best friends.
They ______ in my class.

And that boy over there ______ Bill. He ______ in my class, too, and he ______ very good at maths. In tests he can ______ very useful!

And that girl over there? That ______ my sister! Her name ______ Kate. All her teachers ______ very happy when she ______ ill! And I ______ happy when she ______ back at school again!

And this ______ my baby brother.
His name ______ Timmy.
He ______ three years old.

REGEL

Fragen und Kurzantworten

Is	it	Tom's birthday?	Yes,	it	is.
Is	Jenny	there, too?	No,	she	isn't.
Is	she	ill?	Yes,	she	is.
Are	the children	hungry?	Yes,	they	are.
Are	there	sandwiches on the table?	Yes,	there	are.
Is	that	Tom's baby brother?	Yes,	it	is.
Verb	**Subjekt**			**Subjekt (Pronomen)**	**Verb**

Bei Fragen mit *to be* steht das Verb vor dem Subjekt.
Bei Fragen mit *is there/are there* ist *there* gleichsam das Subjekt der Frage.

Bei Kurzantworten (Antworten, die sich im Deutschen auf ja oder nein beschränken) musst du das Subjekt als Pronomen wiederholen.

Bei einer Antwort mit *yes* steht das Verb in der Langform, bei *no* in der Kurzform.

Auf die Frage *is that* antwortet man mit *Yes, it is/No, it isn' t,* auch wenn nach Personen gefragt wird.

ÜBUNG 3

Your answers

Read through exercise 1 on page 43/44 again. Then give short answers.

1. Is it Timmy's birthday?
2. Is Jenny there?
3. Is Tom eleven years old?
4. Is Jenny Tom's mother?
5. Is Kate Tom's sister?
6. Is that Timmy in the lemonade?
7. Are there sandwiches on the table?
8. Are the children in the bathroom?
9. Are they hungry and thirsty?
10. Is one bottle on the floor?

Go on with other questions and answers.

ÜBUNG 4

A game

At Tom's party the children play a game. They must ask questions and find out what "it" is.
Answer their questions.

Is it a thing?	No, __________
Is it an animal?	No, __________
Is it in this room?	No, __________
Is it a toy?	No, __________
Is it something nice?	No, __________
Is it something terrible?	Yes, __________
Is it a woman?	No, __________
Is it a man?	Yes, __________
Is he old?	Yes, __________
Is he at our school?	Yes, __________
Is it a teacher?	Yes, __________
Is it our maths teacher?	Yes, it is.

REGEL

Fragen mit what, who, where, why und how

Who is Jenny? Who's that?	*who* (= wer) fragt nach Personen.
What is on the table? What's that?	*what* (= was) fragt nach Sachen.
Where is Jenny? Where's she from? Where are you, Timmy?	*where* (= wo) fragt nach einem Ort.
Why isn't Jenny here?	*why* (= warum) fragt nach dem Grund.
How old is she ?	*how* (= wie) fragt in Verbindung mit *old* nach dem Alter.

ÜBUNG 5

Jenny

At the party, Mike wants to know all about Jenny.
He asks Tom a lot of questions. He wants to know

- who Jenny is
- how old she is
- if she is a nice girl
- why she isn't here
- where she is now
- if her parents are at home
- what she has got
- if she has got a temperature
- if she has got brothers and sisters
- if she is from York

Ask Mike's questions.

ÜBUNG 6

Tom's answers

Here are some of Tom's answers. What are the questions?

1. ______________________________

No, she isn't. She's twelve.

2. ______________________________

Yes, she is. She's a very nice girl.

3. ______________________________

Yes, she is. She's my girlfriend.

4. ______________________________

Because she's ill.

5. ______________________________

She's got a cold.

6. ______________________________

No, she hasn't. She hasn't got a temperature.

7. ______________________________

She's at home.

DIKTATE 5 6

Und jetzt solltest du als Abschluss der letzten beiden Kapitel zwei Diktate schreiben. Lass dir die Texte diktieren: Diktat Nr. 5 und Diktat Nr. 6.

8 Die Verlaufsform des Präsens

REGEL

Formen

Bejahte Formen

Langformen		Kurzformen	
I am	talking	I'm	talking
you are	talking	you're	talking
he is	talking	he's	talking
she is	talking	she's	talking
it is	talking	it's	talking
we are	talking	we're	talking
you are	talking	you're	talking
they are	talking	they're	talking

Verneinte Formen

Langformen		Kurzformen	
I am not	talking	I'm not	talking
you are not	talking	you aren't	talking
he is not	talking	he isn't	talking
she is not	talking	she isn't	talking
it is not	talking	it isn't	talking
we are not	talking	we aren't	talking
you are not	talking	you aren't	talking
they are not	talking	they aren't	talking

Das *present progressive* wird mit den Formen von *to be* und einer *ing-form*, dem *present participle* (= Partizip Präsens) gebildet. Das *present progressive* besteht daher immer aus zwei Teilen.

Das *present participle* wird mit dem Infinitiv + *ing* gebildet. Beachte allerdings bei der Bildung:

come	+ ing	coming	Ein auslautendes *-e*, das nicht gesprochen wird, entfällt.
sit	+ ing	sitting	Bei einsilbigen Verben mit kurzem, betontem Vokal wird der auslautende Konsonant verdoppelt.
swim	+ ing	swimming	
lie	+ ing	lying	*ie* wird vor folgendem *-ing* zu *y*.

Auch bei dem *present progressive* – wie bei allen Zeitformen – bestimmt das Subjekt die Form von *to be*, die du gebrauchen musst.

ÜBUNG 1

Present participles

Form the present participles.

come	coming	make	
lie		get	
dry		play	
call		put	
cut		run	
dance		sit	
drink		swim	
fly		tie	
listen		watch	

ÜBUNG 2

At Tom's party

At Tom's party all the children are busy. What are they doing?

1. Mike/take/photos.
2. John/sit at the kitchen table/and drink/all the lemonade.
3. Kate/skip.
4. Tom/ring up/Jenny.
5. Betty/flirt/with Kevin.
6. Some boys/play/football in the kitchen.
7. Some girls/dance/in the kitchen.
8. Ann/lie on the floor/and watch/a film on TV.
9. Jim and Barbara/eat/sandwiches.
10. Susan/sit in a corner/and read a magazine.

ÜBUNG 3 **Timmy's "report"**

Timmy is at the party, too, but he's very small and Tom doesn't want to have him there. So he tells him to go to his mother. Timmy goes and tells his mum that

1. Mike is playing with his camera.
2. John is eating all the sandwiches.
3. Kate is hopping around like a rabbit.
4. Tom is talking to his teacher.
5. Betty is talking nonsense to Kevin.
6. some boys are quarrelling about a ball.
7. some girls are running around in the kitchen.
8. Ann is lying on the floor because she is ill.
9. Jim and Barbara are making sandwiches.
10. Susan is reading my picture book.

Can you correct Timmy?

Example: That's not right, Timmy. Mike isn't playing with his camera, he's taking photos.

REGEL

Fragen und Kurzantworten

	Are	you	talking	to your teacher?
	Is	Jenny	lying	in bed?
What	are	you	doing,	Tom?

Bei Fragen im *present progressive* steht zunächst eine Form von *to be,* dann das Subjekt und schließlich das *present participle.*
Fragewörter wie *why, where, when, what* werden einfach vor die Form von *to be* gesetzt. Die Wortstellung ändert sich dadurch nicht.

No,	I	'm not.	Pronomen + Kurzform (verneinte Form)
Yes,	I	am.	Pronomen + Langform (bejahte Form)
Yes,	she	is.	
No,	she	isn't.	

Bei den Kurzantworten wird das *present participle* ausgelassen.
Ansonsten gelten die bereits bekannten Regeln.
Bei Fragen mit Fragewörtern sind keine Kurzantworten möglich.
What are you doing, Tom? – I'm talking to Jenny.

ÜBUNG 4 Timmy's questions

When Timmy's mother hears what Timmy says, she thinks that he is wrong. So she asks him some questions. Ask her questions and give Timmy's answers.

Example: Is Mike really playing with his camera? – Yes, he is.
Is John really eating all the sandwiches? ...

Go on.

ÜBUNG 5 Timmy's questions

Timmy's mother still thinks that he's wrong, so she sends him back. She wants to know

- what Kate is doing,
- if Tom is really talking to his teacher,
- what Mike is doing with his camera,
- if Susan is really reading his picture book,
- why Ann is lying on the floor,
- if Kate is playing a new game,
- what the boys are doing with the ball,
- what the girls are doing in the kitchen,
- what John is doing,
- what Jim and Barbara are doing.

Now you are Timmy. Ask Timmy's questions and give the answers.

Example: What are you doing, Kate? – I'm skipping.

ÜBUNG 6 In Timmy's room

First scene:
<u>At 7.30</u> the party is over. The children are going <u>home</u>. They are all <u>happy</u>. <u>Timmy</u> is happy, too. He is <u>in his room</u>. He is lying <u>on the floor</u>, but he isn't <u>crying</u>. <u>He's</u> playing with Tom's birthday presents. They are <u>in his room</u> now. One parcel is open. There's a picture book and some chocolate in it.

Second scene:
Timmy is still lying <u>on the floor</u>. There is chocolate on his face and hands. He isn't playing any more. He's got <u>a pencil</u> in his hand and he is drawing <u>a picture</u> in Tom's picture book.

Third scene:
Somebody is coming upstairs. He is shouting a name. It is Timmy's brother. He is looking for his presents. He is angry. He is opening the door of Timmy's room. But the room is empty. Where is Timmy? Can you see him?

Read through the text, then ask about the underlined words. Be careful with the question words. Remember:

who?	–	wer?
where?	–	wo, wohin?
what?	–	was?
when?	–	wann?
why?	–	warum, wieso?
how?	–	wie?

DIKTAT 7

Und jetzt solltest du als Abschluss dieses Kapitels ein kurzes Diktat schreiben. Lass dir den Text diktieren: Diktat Nr. 7. In dem Diktat kommt ein Wort vor, das du vielleicht noch nicht kennst:

hole [həʊl] – Loch

Sieh dir das Wort gut an.

9 Modale Hilfsverben

After the party Kate can go to her room. It isn't her birthday, so she needn't help. But Tom must. He must help his mother to wash up the dishes and clean the kitchen floor. Then they must tidy up the living-room.
Must Timmy help, too? No, he needn't. He must go to bed because it's already late. He is very unhappy. "Why can't I help you? Why must I always go to bed?" he cries. "Look, Timmy," his mother says, "It's already 8 o'clock; you must go to bed now. You can stay up longer next year." But Timmy is still unhappy. "I can wash the dishes, too." "OK, Timmy, you can help Tom with the dishes, but you mustn't drop them," his mother says. "Fetch the dirty plates from the living-room," Tom says to him. Timmy is happy now. He is big and strong and he can help. But what's that? There is a loud noise in the living-room, then everything is quiet again. When Tom opens the door, Timmy is gone, but there are three plates on the floor ...

Schau dir den Text genau an. Die unterstrichenen Verben sind so genannte modale Hilfsverben.

ACHTUNG

Modale Hilfsverben gibt es auch im Deutschen. Es entsprechen dabei:

can	können, dürfen
can't	nicht können, nicht dürfen
mustn't	nicht dürfen
must	müssen
needn't	nicht müssen, nicht brauchen

Für „dürfen" bzw. „nicht dürfen" kann in Fragen und Kurzantworten auch *may* (statt *can*) bzw. *may not* (statt *mustn' t, can' t*) stehen:

Yes, you may.

May I help you?

No, you may not.

Englische Hilfsverben weisen folgende Eigenschaften auf:

1. Sie haben keinen Infinitiv und kein *-s* in der 3. Person Singular.
2. Ihre Formen sind für alle Personen gleich.
3. Hilfsverben können im Englischen nicht alleine stehen; ihnen muss immer ein Verb folgen (eine Ausnahme bilden die Kurzantworten). Vergleiche:

   Er kann Englisch. He can speak English.

4. Wie im Deutschen folgt einem Hilfsverb immer ein Infinitiv.
5. Objekte und andere Ergänzungen stehen im Englischen immer nach der Verbgruppe. Vergleiche:

   Er kann sie sehen. He can see her.

ÜBUNG 1 **Timmy**

Complete the sentences.

Timmy is three.

1. He __________ go to school.	1. Er braucht nicht …
2. He __________ go to kindergarten.	2. Er kann …
3. He ________ play with other children there.	3. Er kann …
4. __________ he go there every day?	4. Muss er …?
5. No, he __________ .	5. Nein, er muss nicht.
6. __________ he go there alone?	6. Darf er …?
7. No, he __________ .	7. Nein, er darf nicht.
8. __________ he take his bike?	8. Darf er …?
9. No, he __________ . It's too dangerous.	9. Nein, er darf nicht.
10. ________ Tom fetch him in the afternoon?	10. Muss Tom …
11. Yes, he _______ on Thursdays and Fridays.	11. Ja, er muss …

ÜBUNG 2 **Right or wrong?**

Look at the text again, then correct the wrong statements.

1. Kate must go to her room. – No, that's wrong. Kate can go to her room.

1. Kate must go to her room.
2. She mustn't help her mother.
3. Tom must clean Kate's room.
4. He needn't wash up the dishes.
5. He must clean the kitchen floor.
6. He must clean the kitchen windows, too.
7. Timmy can help him.
8. Timmy must clean the kitchen floor, too.
9. Timmy must drop the plates.
10. Timmy can stay up a little longer.

ÜBUNG 3 **A phone call**

The next day, Tom rings up Jenny again. Jenny's mother answers the phone.

Tom	*Jenny's mother*
1. __________ I talk to Jenny, please?	1. Sorry, Tom, you __________ Jenny's in the bathroom.
2. __________ Jenny come to school tomorrow?	2. No, she __________ . She __________ get up.
3. __________ she stay in bed all day?	3. Yes, she __________ .
4. __________ she take medicine?	4. No, she __________ .
5. __________ I see her this afternoon?	5. No, you __________ see her today. She __________ go to the doctor's.

ÜBUNG 4 What Jenny must do

When Tom rings up again, Jenny tells him what she must or mustn't do.

Begin: I must/mustn't …

1. Don't go to school.
2. Stay in bed.
3. Don't watch too much TV.
4. Take your temperature every morning.
5. Take your medicine.
6. Come to my surgery again on Monday at 4 o'clock.
7. Don't play with your friends.

ÜBUNG 5 Jenny is really ill

What can, must, needn't, mustn't Jenny do?

take her medicine
watch TV
ride her bike
read a book
go to school
clean her room
do her homework
help her mother in the kitchen
ring up her friends
listen to music
write letters
play football

ÜBUNG 6

Good patients

Correct the following statements. One sentence is already correct.

1. A good patient can do what the doctor tells him/her.
2. A good patient mustn't tell the doctor what he/she has got.
3. A good patient mustn't take any medicine.
4. A good patient needn't stay in bed when he/she is ill.
5. A good patient must clean the doctor's car.
6. A good patient can forget his/her appointment.
7. A good patient mustn't be late at the doctor's surgery.
8. A good patient mustn't listen to his/her doctor.
9. A good patient must clean the doctor's surgery.

REGEL

Fragen und Kurzantworten

Can	Kate	get up?	Yes,	she	can.
			No,	she	can't.
Must	she	stay in bed?	Yes,	she	must.
			No,	she	needn't.
Hilfsverb	**Subjekt**	**Infinitiv**		**Pronomen**	**Hilfsverb**

Bei Fragen steht das Hilfsverb vor dem Subjekt; nach dem Subjekt steht immer der Infinitiv.
Bei Kurzfragen wird nur das Hilfsverb wiederholt; die verneinte Form von *must* ist *needn' t*.

ÜBUNG 7 At the doctor's

When you are ill, you can ask your doctor a lot of questions. Can you give the doctor's answers?

1. Must I go to school? — No, ________________
2. Must I do my homework? — No, ________________
3. Must I stay in bed all day? — Yes, ________________
4. Can I get up? — No, ________________
5. Can I ring up my friends? — Yes, ________________
6. Must I take my temperature? — Yes, ________________
7. May my friends come to see me? — Yes, ________________, but not on the first day.
8. Can I watch TV? — Yes, ________________
9. Must I take all that medicine? — Yes, ________________

ÜBUNG 8 Your questions

One of your friends is ill. You go and see her and you ask her

– if she is very ill	(Yes)
– if she must stay in bed	(Yes)
– if she must stay indoors all day	(Yes)
– if she may get up for an hour or two	(Yes)
– if she has got a temperature	(Yes)
– if she can go to school on Thursday	(No)
– if she is happy that she needn't go to school	(Yes)
– if her teachers are happy, too	(No)

Ask the questions and answer them.

REGEL

Shall I ...? / Shall we ...?

Shall	I	open	the window for you?	Soll ich ...?
Shall	I	give	you your medicine?	Soll ich ...?
Shall	we	call	the doctor again?	Sollen wir...?

***Shall* + Subj.+ Infinitiv**

Zu den modalen Hilfsverben gehört auch *shall*. Mit *Shall I / Shall we ...?* kann man einen Wunsch erfragen oder ein Angebot machen. Allerdings ist dies nur mit *I* und *we* möglich.

ÜBUNG 9 **Helping people**

Your mother is ill. What can you do for her? Here are some ideas:

Example: Shall I do the shopping for you?

do the washing-up

do the shopping

clean the rooms

make her bed

go to the chemist's

make her some tea

get her medicine

cook the meals

open the window

ring up the doctor

look after my sister/brother

Das Präsens von Vollverben

10

Vollverben sind Verben, die eine Tätigkeit oder einen Zustand nennen oder beschreiben. Sie kommen im Englischen wie im Deutschen in verschiedenen Zeiten *(= tenses)* vor. Eine dieser Zeiten ist das *simple present:*

REGEL

Bejahte Formen

I	like	ice cream.	
You	like	sweets.	
My father	likes	tennis.	• In der 3. Person Singular *(he, she, it)* wird ein *-s* angehängt.
My mother	likes	English.	
A cat	likes	mice.	
We	like	Tom.	• Bis auf die 3. Person Singular hat das Präsens damit die gleiche Form wie der Infinitiv (ohne *to*).
You	like	us.	
They	like	TV.	

ACHTUNG

Besonderheiten bei der Schreibung

He always catches the bus at six o'clock. He sometimes misses it.	• Bei Verben, die auf einen Zischlaut enden, hängt man ein *-es* [ɪz] an, wenn sie nicht auf *-e* enden.
He goes home. He does his homework.	• Auch bei *to go* und *to do* wird in der 3. Person Singular ein *-es* angehängt.
to fly — He flies to France. to try — He tries to be helpful. aber: to stay — He stays at home.	• Wie bei der Pluralbildung der Substantive ändert sich das *-y* nach einem Vokal nicht; nach einem Konsonant wird es jedoch zu *-ies*.

ÜBUNG 1 **What Tom does**

Use the simple present.

1. He ________________ at 7 o'clock every morning. (get up)
2. Then he ________________ and ________________ on his clothes. (wash/put)
3. Then he ________________ down to the dining-room. (go)
4. There he ________________ breakfast. (have)
5. Then he ________________ for his schoolbag. (look)
6. After that he ________________ the house. (leave)
7. Then he ________________ to the bus stop. (go)
8. He usually ________________ the bus when it is cold. (take)
9. He ________________ at school at a quarter to nine. (arrive)

ÜBUNG 2 **Before lessons begin**

TALK COPY RUN MAKE CLEAN DO WRITE EAT PLAY

a) Complete the sentences with the verbs in the cloud.

1. Mike and Tom ______________ football in the classroom.
2. Sam ______________ his sandwiches.
3. Sandra ______________ her English homework.
4. Anne ______________ to Betty.
5. John ______________ his homework from his neighbour.
6. Kevin ______________ around in the classroom.
7. Bob and David ______________ a lot of noise, too.
8. Pam ______________ the board.
9. Jane and Sharon ______________ letters.

b) What do you usually do before lessons begin? Write down five sentences.

REGEL

Verneinte Formen

I	don't	like	maths.
You	don't	like	biology.
Tom	doesn't	like	maths.
Jenny	doesn't	like	English.
We	don't	like	our teacher.
You	don't	like	geography.
They	don't	like	their teacher.
Subjekt	***don't/doesn't***	**Infinitiv *(no -s !)***	

Bei der Verneinung musst du eine Form von *to do* gebrauchen. Diese Form lautet in der 3. Person Singular *doesn' t (= does not)*, in den anderen Personen *don' t (= do not)*. Das folgende Verb steht im Infinitiv, d. h. du darfst in der dritten Person kein *-s* oder-*es* anhängen.

ACHTUNG

Ist *to do* ein Vollverb, so heißt die Verneinung *don' t do/doesn' t do*:

He doesn't do his homework.
They don't do their homework.

ÜBUNG 3 **A strange family**

The Browns live in Tom's neighbourhood. They have got four children. Say what they don't do.

1. They ___don't get up___ in the morning. (get up)
2. They ________________ an early breakfast. (have)
3. Mr Brown ________________ his car. (wash)
4. Mrs Brown ________________ the cooking. (do)
5. Often, their children ________________ to school. (go)
6. They ________________ school. (like)
7. Helen ________________ her teachers. (like)
8. She ________________ her homework. (do)

ÜBUNG 4

People are different

Example: Tom likes bananas, but he doesn't like oranges.

Tom		Jenny + Kate		Timmy		Mike		The Browns	
bananas	+	volleyball	+	cornflakes	+	photos	+	work	–
oranges	–	tennis	–	tea	–	comics	–	sleeping	+
Jenny	+	sports	+	dogs	+	music	+	books	–
Ben	–	all sports	–	cats	–	singing	–	TV	+

ÜBUNG 5

Over to you

What do you/your friends/your parents like? What don't you/don't they like?

Example: I like football, but my father doesn't. He likes tennis.

Go on. Write down five sentences.

REGEL

Fragen und Kurzantworten

Do	you	like	football?	– Yes, I do. – No, I don't.
Does	your mother	like	football, too?	– Yes, she does. – No, she doesn't.
Form von *to do*	**Subjekt *(no -s /-es)***	**Infinitiv**	**Pronomen**	**Form von *to do***

Bei Fragen mit einem Vollverb musst du immer eine Form von *to do* gebrauchen. Wie bei der Verneinung steht das Verb im Infinitiv.

In der Kurzantwort steht für das Vollverb immer eine Form von *to do*.

Aufgepasst:

Do you always do your homework? — Yes, I do.
Do you often do it in the morning? — No, I don't.

Wenn *to do* ein Vollverb ist, muss es auch bei Fragen wiederholt werden.

ÜBUNG 6 Mike

Mike is new in Tom's class. The first day his new classmates ask him a lot of questions.

__________ you like it here?

__________ your mother like York?

__________ you like English?

__________ you like school?

__________ you play hockey?

__________ you go to school by bike?

__________ you like sports?

__________ your sister go to our school, too?

__________ you play an instrument?

__________ your father work in York?

ÜBUNG 7 Can you ask the questions?

A reporter for the school magazine asks Mike a lot of questions, too. What are they?

1. ____________________? Yes, I really like it. It's a nice class.
2. ____________________? No, I don't like all subjects.
3. ____________________? No, I don't. I really don't like maths.
4. ____________________? No, I don't like all the teachers.
5. ____________________? No, I don't forget my homework very often.
6. ____________________? No, I don't come to school by bus, I come on my bike.
7. ____________________? No. In winter I take the bus.
8. ____________________? No, I don't play football.
9. ____________________? Yes. My parents live here, too.
10. ____________________? Yes. I usually do my homework in the afternoon.

REGEL

Fragen mit Fragewörtern

When	does	Mike	get	up?
When	do	his parents	get	up?
What	do	they	do	then?
Why	does	Mike	get	up at 7?
How	does	his sister	go	to school?
When	do	his parents	take	him there?
What subjects	doesn't	he	like?	
Fragewort	**Form von *to do***	**Subjekt**	**Infinitiv**	

Die Wortstellung: „Form von *to do* + Subjekt + Infinitiv" bleibt auch dann erhalten, wenn die Frage mit einem Fragewort beginnt.

ACHTUNG

To do muss wiederholt werden, wenn es ein Vollverb ist:

What does Mike do in the evenings?
What do you do at school?

ÜBUNG 8

An interview

Ask your friend and give his/her answers.

1. Where/you/live?
2. When/get up/in the morning?
3. When/your mother/get up?
4. What/have/for breakfast?
5. Why/not like/cornflakes?
6. When/your parents/leave the house?
7. When/they/come home again?
8. How/get/to school?
9. Why/not take/the bus?
10. What/do/in the afternoon?
11. What games/do/like?
12. What/do/in the evening?
13. When/go/to bed?
14. When/switch off/the light?
15. When/your parents/go to bed?

ÜBUNG 9

Mike's father

a) Can you make up an interview with Mike's father?

1. He gets up at 5.30 o'clock in the morning.	When ________ you ____________?
2. He starts work at seven o'clock.	When ____________________?
3. He leaves his house at 6.30.	When ____________________?
4. He drives a school bus.	What ____________________?
5. He collects the children from the villages.	Who ____________________?
6. He takes them to school.	Where ____________________?
7. School starts at a quarter to nine.	When ____________________?
8. In the afternoon he fetches them from school.	When ____________________?
9. He takes them home again.	Where ____________________?
10. Then he cleans the bus.	What ____________________?
11. He often finds things in the bus.	What ____________________?

b) Write down what Mike's father does.

Begin like this: I get up at 5.30 because work …

DIKTAT 8

Und jetzt solltest du als Abschluss dieses Kapitels ein kurzes Diktat schreiben. Lass dir den Text diktieren – Diktat Nr. 8.

In dem Diktat kommen zwei Wörter vor, die du vielleicht noch nicht kennst:

single parent – Alleinerziehende(r)
part-time job – Teilzeitarbeit

11 Die einfache Gegenwart und die Verlaufsform im Vergleich

REGEL

Present progressive

Look! Mike is doing his homework.
He's doing a German exercise now.

Das *present progressive* gebraucht man für Handlungen, die zur Zeit des Sprechens noch nicht vorbei sind, sondern noch ablaufen.
Signalwörter dafür sind: *now, at this moment, look, listen, today, this morning (afternoon, evening)* etc.

Simple present

He always does his homework after school.
He goes to a comprehensive school.

Das *simple present* gebraucht man für wiederholte, gewohnheitsmäßige und lang andauernde Handlungen.
Signalwörter sind hier: *always, often, sometimes, never, usually, every day (week, month, year), in the morning (afternoon, evening)* etc.
Die Signalwörter stehen meist vor dem Hauptverb.

ÜBUNG 1 **Things are different today**

Use the simple present or the present progressive.

1. Mike usually ________________ up at 7, but today he is still in bed. He ________________ .
2. He usually ________________ breakfast at 7. 30, but today he ________________ in bed.

get
sleep
have
still – lie

3. He often ________________ little time to spend in the	have
bathroom, but this morning he ________________ a bath.	take
4. He usually ________________ on his school uniform, but	put
today he ________________ his other clothes.	wear
5. He usually ________________ lunch at school, but today	have
he ________________ lunch at home.	
6. Mike usually ________________ his mother with the	help
dishes, but today he needn't.	
His father ________________ the dishes.	wash
7. His parents usually ________________ in the afternoon,	work
but things are different today. They ________________ for	go
a walk. Do you know why?	
Well, it's ________________ .	

ÜBUNG 2

What about your Sundays?

What do you always/often/never/usually/sometimes do on Sundays?
Here are some ideas:

On Sundays I	always never usually sometimes often	get up late play football watch TV clean my bike clean my room ring up my friends cook lunch go for a walk help Mum und Dad brush my shoes do my homework learn English write letters go to school visit relatives listen to cassettes

ÜBUNG 3 Mike's hobby

Use the simple present or the present progressive.

1. Mike ______________ a picture of his new school. He	take
______________ taking pictures.	like
2. He ______________ only ______________ pictures of	take
schools, he ______________ pictures of everything.	
Here he ______________ a picture of Tom and Jenny.	
3. He always ______________ his pictures in an album.	put
Look! He ______________ a picture in his album now.	
4. He ______________ already ______________ a lot of	have got
albums. He ______________ them in his room.	keep

ÜBUNG 4 Mike's photos

Here are some of Mike's photos. Can you complete the text?

This is Dad.
sit/bus

This is Dad again.
clean/bus

This is our house.
live/there now

This is Mum.
leave the house/
always leave at 8

This is our garden.
Look! Mum/work
in it/like her garden

This is our corner shop.
Mum/work there/
sell groceries

REGEL

Das simple present für aufeinander folgende Handlungen

After school Mike often goes to see Tom. When they arrive at Tom's, they first put their schoolbags in a corner. Then they go to the kitchen and look for something to drink. Then they go to Tom's room. There they play for an hour or two. After that they do their homework together. Then Mike goes home.

Das *simple present* steht im Englischen auch für aufeinander folgende Handlungen. Solche Handlungen kommen vor allem in Erzählungen und Berichten vor. Signalwörter sind *first, then, after that, next, soon, at last* etc.

ÜBUNG 5

Scrambled eggs

Today Tom's and Kate's parents are out, but the children are very hungry. So they go into the kitchen and try to find something to eat. But the fridge is empty. There are only some eggs in it, so they try to make scrambled eggs. Connect the sentences and put them in the correct order. Use words like "first, now, then".

take the eggs upstairs

put the pan on the oven

break the eggs

eat them

put the eggs in a bowl

put fat in it

look for a frying pan

stir the eggs

put scrambled eggs on a plate

add some milk, salt and pepper

stir two or three times

put every-thing in the frying pan

scrambled eggs	– Rührеier	oven	– Ofen
fridge	– Kühlschrank	fat	– Fett
frying pan	– Bratpfanne	to stir	– umrühren

ÜBUNG 6 Mr Mason

Usually Tom's and Kate's parents are home in the evening, but both work and so sometimes they are late. Tom's father is a vet. Here's a day in his life.

7^{00}	get up at seven o'clock
$7^{00}-7^{30}$	wash
7^{30}	have breakfast
8^{00}	get in his car
8^{30}	open his surgery
$9^{00}-12^{00}$	examine sick animals
12^{30}	have lunch at a restaurant
13^{45}	leave restaurant
17^{00}	have a cup of tea
17^{30}	close the door of the surgery
18^{00}	get home

a) Make up an interview. Ask Mr Mason what he usually does.

Example: When do you usually have breakfast?

b) Write down what Mr Mason does every day. Use signal words.

ÜBUNG 7 What you do

Write about your day. Use signal words like *first, then,* etc.

ÜBUNG 8

Another breakfast

Use the simple present or the present progressive.

The weather is fine and the sun ________________ (shine). It is already ten o'clock, and the Masons ________________ still ________________ (sit) at the breakfast table. Nobody ________________ (do) any work. Mr Mason ________________ (not look) after animals and Mrs Mason – she ________________ (work) in a hospital as a nurse – ________________ (not look) after her patients.

It's Sunday. The Masons always ________________ (have) a late breakfast on Sundays. But somebody is missing. It's Kate. She is still in her room; she ____________________ (sleep). "Where's Kate?" Mr Mason ________________ (ask). "What ________________ she ________________ (do) in her room? Well, Timmy, go and get her."

So Timmy ________________ (go) to Kate's room. He ________________ (open) the door and ________________ (see) that Kate is still in her bed. He ________________ (try) to wake her up, but Kate ________________ (not listen), so Timmy ________________ (go) back and ________________ (tell) his dad that Kate ________________ still ________________ (sleep). "Haven't you got a water-pistol, Tom?" Mr Mason ________________ (say). "Come on, Timmy. Get it and ask your sister if she ________________ (not want) to get up now."

So Timmy ______________ (fetch) Tom's water-pistol and ______________ (go) to Kate's room. Suddenly there is a loud noise in Kate's room and somebody ______________ (shout) in an angry voice: "You just wait, Timmy!"

DIKTAT 9

Und jetzt solltest du als Abschluss dieses Kapitels ein kurzes Diktat schreiben. Lass dir den Text diktieren – Diktat Nr. 9.

12 Fragen, Kurzantworten und die Verneinung im Überblick

In the English lesson Tom sometimes writes letters to Jenny. Here is one of his letters, but somebody has changed it:

Dear Jenny,
I hope we can**'t** see each other this afternoon. I have**n't** got a lot of homework to do, but I **don't** think I can come at 4 o'clock. Can you wait for me at the bus stop? I hope I can**'t** come. I really **don't** want to see you again. You are**n't** the nicest girl I know. I am **not** always thinking of you. You know I **don't** like you.

Love, **(ha! ha!)**

Tom

REGEL

Die Verneinung

Wenn du diesen Brief anschaust, siehst du, dass die Verneinung im Englischen nur bei Vollverben im *simple present* mit einer Form von *to do* (= *do not/does not* bzw. *don' t/doesn' t*) gebildet wird. Bei den Formen von *to be*, *have got*, den Hilfsverben *can*, *may* etc. und dem *present progressive* wird die Verneinung nur mit *not* gebildet.

ÜBUNG 1 **Tom's letter**

Write Tom's letter again and correct it.

ÜBUNG 2 **What is right?**

What do you think is right?

When Jenny gets Tom's letter,

all her neighbours begin to laugh
she is very unhappy
she falls ill
she is very angry with him
she kicks Tom
she reads it to the class
she shows it to her teacher
she must leave the classroom
she writes a letter, too
she must laugh
she goes home immediately
she begins to cry

Example: Jenny doesn't begin to cry.

ÜBUNG 3 **Jenny**

Make up Jenny's portrait.

Example: Jenny hasn't got a sister, but she has got a baby brother.

not a sister, a baby brother	Jenny – not ten, twelve years	her parents a flat, not a house	her father a van, not a car
to school not by bus, but by bike	like maths, not English	a good maths teacher, awful English teacher	not like all boys in her class, but Tom
sometimes late, but not often	like music, not like singing	can play a lot of games, but not football	good at volley-ball, bad at swimming

ÜBUNG 4 Another portrait

Make up your own or a friend's portrait. Use negative forms, too.

ÜBUNG 5 Good pupils

What's your idea of a good pupil? Here are some ideas to help you. Correct the sentences that are wrong. Use negative forms.

- Good pupils always talk to their teachers.
- Good pupils are silly.
- Good pupils never forget anything.
- Good pupils have got a lot of friends.
- Good pupils never make their teachers angry.
- Good pupils never talk in lessons.
- Good pupils are unhappy.
- Good pupils are bad at sports.
- Good pupils always do their homework.
- Good pupils work too much.

REGEL

Die Fragebildung

Does	Tom	like Jenny?	Is	Tom		happy?
Do	his parents	like her?	Has	he	got	a girlfriend?
			Is	he	writing	her a letter?
			Can	he	see	her?
Hilfsverb	**Subjekt**	**Verb**	**Hilfsverb**	**Subjekt**	**Verb**	

ACHTUNG

Bei Fragen mit Formen von *to be, have got* oder Hilfsverben wie *can, must* etc. wird keine Form von *to do* gebraucht.

Auch im *present progressive* wird die Frageform nicht mit *to do* gebildet.

ÜBUNG 6 An article for the school magazine

Tom is in his room. He is writing an article about pupils who are unhappy at school. He tries to make up a kind of test for his readers to see if they are happy or not. He wants to know if they

are often alone
like their parents
have got any friends
have got any hobbies
parents often play with them
have got anybody to talk to
watch a lot of TV
most of their teachers are nice
are often afraid
often cry
can do what they want
their parents are often out in the evening

Can you help Tom to ask the questions?

Example: Are you often alone?

ÜBUNG 7 You and your school

Complete the sentences.

________ you ________________ school?	like
________ you often ________________ your homework?	forget
________ you ________________ your homework now?	do
________ your mum ________________ you now?	help
________ your parents often ________________ you?	help
________ you ________________ nice teachers?	have got
________ they ________________ you?	like

________ they ________	you a lot of homework?		give
________ you ________	during lessons?		can talk
________ you ________	chewing gum in the English lessons?		may eat
________ you ________	a school magazine at your school?		have got
________ you ________	it?		read
________ you ________	it interesting?		find

ÜBUNG 8 **Pupils, pupils ...**

As you know, there are different kinds of pupils. There are pupils who

- find everything boring
- often sleep during lessons
- are often late

- are often ill for tests
- only like sports

- can't sit still
- talk all the time
- can't listen

- listen only when the teacher gets angry
- often forget things
- don't do their homework

Find out what kind of pupil your friend is.
Make up a list of questions you can ask him/her.

REGEL

Entscheidungsfragen und Kurzantworten

Bei Fragen musst du zwischen zwei Grundtypen unterscheiden, nämlich zwischen Entscheidungsfragen und Ergänzungsfragen. Bei Entscheidungsfragen will man wissen, ob sich eine Sache so oder so verhält. Man antwortet daher immer mit ja oder nein. Im Englischen entspricht diesem ja oder nein eine Kurzantwort. Vergleiche:

to be:	Is	Kate	ill?	Yes, she No, she	is. isn't.
present progressive:	Is	she	sleeping?	Yes, she No, she	is. isn't.
auxiliary:	Must	she	see a doctor?	Yes, she No, she	must. needn't.
have got:	Has	she	got a cold?	Yes, she No, she	has. hasn't.
simple present:	Does	she	go to school?	Yes, she No, she	does. doesn't.
	Do	her friends	look after her?	Yes, they No, they	do. don't.
	Hilfsverb	**Subjekt**	**Verb**	**Subjekt (Pronomen)**	**Hilfsverb**

Merke:
– Für Vollverben im *simple present* tritt eine Form von *to do* ein.
– Das Subjekt der Kurzantwort ist immer ein Pronomen (*I, you* etc.).
– Nach *yes* steht eine Langform, nach *no* die Kurzform.

Is this your brother?	Yes, it is.
Is that your mother?	Yes, it is.

Ist *this* oder *that* das Subjekt des Fragesatzes, so steht in der Kurzantwort immer *it*.

ÜBUNG 9

Timmy's new picture book

While Tom is writing in his room, the door opens and Timmy comes in. He has got a new picture book and a lot of questions. Can you answer them? Give short answers.

1. Look at that house, Tom. Is that a church?
2. The man with the hat – is that a postman?
3. And what is he doing? Is he trying to get into the house?
4. And what about those men? Are they climbing the ladder?
5. Or are they running away?
6. Is the man running after the two other men?
7. Does he want to catch them?
8. Are they afraid of him?
9. Is he a policeman?
10. Do they want to steal the bike?
11. Do they want to ride away on it?
12. Is that a bike, too?

REGEL

Ergänzungsfragen

Im Unterschied zu Entscheidungsfragen will man bei Ergänzungsfragen eine zusätzliche Information über eine Sache oder eine Person. Ergänzungsfragen beginnen daher immer mit einem Fragewort. Solche Fragewörter sind im Englischen:

who	(wer/wen)	fragt nach Personen
what	(was)	fragt nach Sachen
whose	(wessen)	fragt nach dem Besitzer
why	(warum)	fragt nach dem Grund
where	(wo/wohin)	fragt nach dem Ort oder der Richtung
when	(wann)	fragt nach der Zeit
how	(wie)	fragt nach dem Wie

Nach Ergänzungsfragen sind Kurzantworten mit *yes* oder *no* nicht möglich!

Bei Ergänzungsfragen musst du beachten, ob du nach dem Subjekt eines Satzes oder nach anderen Satzteilen fragen willst.

a) Fragen nach dem Subjekt

Who	has got	a new pet?	Jenny has.
Who	must look	after it?	Jenny must.
Who	is looking	after it?	Jenny is.
Who	buys	its food?	Jenny does.
Who	doesn't pay	for its food?	Jenny doesn't.
Whose dad	pays	for it?	Jenny's dad does.
Subjekt			**Subjekt**

Bei der Frage nach dem Subjekt steht das Fragewort an der Stelle des Subjekts. *To do* wird deshalb nur in verneinten Fragen gebraucht. Diese Regeln gelten auch für das Fragepronomen *what*, wenn man nach dem Subjekt fragt (z. B. *What is lying on the table? What is happening?*).

Bei Fragen nach dem Subjekt steht das Verb – wie auch im Deutschen – immer in der 3. Person Singular:

Who is coming?
Who is ill?
Who has got a pet?

b) Fragen nach anderen Satzteilen

Bei Fragen nach anderen Satzteilen als dem Subjekt gelten die bereits bekannten Regeln:

Fragewort	Hilfsverb	Subjekt	Verb
Where	are	you?	
What	are	you	doing?
Who	are	you	ringing up?
What	has	she	got?
What	must	she	do?
When	must	she	go?
What	does	she	say?
Who	does	she	help?
Where	does	she	go?

Bei Fragen mit Formen von *to be, have got* oder Hilfsverben wie *can, must* etc. wird keine Form von *to be* gebraucht. (Vgl. S. 76)

To do ist nur bei Vollverben im *simple present* möglich.

ACHTUNG

Mit *who* (wer/wen) und *what* (was) kannst du sowohl nach dem Subjekt als auch nach dem Objekt fragen.

Who likes Tom? (= Wer mag Tom?)
Who does Tom like? (= Wen mag Tom?)

ÜBUNG 10 **Jenny**

Ask about the underlined words.

1. <u>Jenny</u> is Tom's girlfriend.
2. <u>Her parents</u> are from Leeds.
3. They have got <u>a car</u>.
4. Sometimes <u>her parents</u> are strict (= streng).
5. She can't always see <u>Tom</u>.
6. She must tell her parents <u>where she is going</u>.
7. <u>She</u> must be back <u>early</u>.
8. She mustn't be out after 8 o'clock <u>in the evening</u>.
9. Listen! <u>The telephone</u> is ringing.
10. Tom is <u>at home</u>.

ÜBUNG 11 A telephone call

Jenny wants to tell Tom some news, but the line is bad. So Tom must ask a lot of questions.

Example: Jenny: "I've got a new pet." Tom: "What have you got?"

1. "I've got a new pet."	1. "What ______________?"
2. "A new pet. It's a hamster."	2. "What ______________?"
3. "I like it."	3. "What ______________?"
4. "I must buy some food for it."	4. "What ______________?"
5. "Food. Can you come to the pet shop?"	5. "Where______________?"
6. "Can you lend me some money?"	6. "What must ______________?"
7. "I want to buy a book about hamsters, too."	7. "What ______________?"
8. "A book about hamsters. I don't know anything about hamsters."	8. "I can't understand you. The line is very bad."
9. " ______________?"	9. "The line. I can't understand you."
10. " ______________?"	10. "You. Let's meet at the pet shop then."
11. "At the pet shop? Yes, OK, at three o'clock."	11. "OK. See you then."

ÜBUNG 12

Bingo

Jenny and Tom meet at the pet shop. They buy a book and some food for Jenny's new pet. Then they go for a walk in the park. There they see two girls and a man with a dog. His name is Bingo.

The girls ask the man a lot of questions about the dog. Here are the man's answers. What are their questions?

1. How old ____________________? Hc's nearly two years old.
2. Where ____________________? He sleeps in the hall.
3. When ____________________? I usually get up at six.
4. What ____________________? Then I make him his breakfast.
5. What ____________________? Usually, he has some dog food.
6. When ____________________? Well, I take him for a walk after breakfast.
7. When ____________________? I go to work at half past eight.
8. Where ____________________? I take him to my neighbour's house.
9. How long ____________________? He stays there until I come home.
10. Where ____________________? We play in the garden.
11. What ____________________? I try to teach him some tricks.
12. What ____________________? In the evening? Well, we watch TV together.
13. What films ____________________? He likes westerns.
14. Why ____________________? Well, he likes horses.

ÜBUNG 13

Making a date

Before Tom and Jenny go home again, they try to make a date. What are Tom's questions?

Where? What? Why? How long? When?

1. can see/again/you/I
2. we/meet again/can
3. you/stay/can
4. must/back/be/you
5. back/be/you/so early/must
6. must/your mother/help/you
7. must/do/you

13 Das will- und going to-Futur

REGEL

Das will-future

What will happen next year?	Kate will be twelve.
When will she be twelve?	She'll be twelve in May.
Will she be happy then?	Yes, she will.
Will she be unhappy?	No, she won't.

Das *will-future* wird mit *will + Infinitiv* (bei Kurzformen: mit *'ll + Infinitiv*) gebildet. Verneinte Formen bildet man mit *will not + Infinitiv* (Kurzform: *won't + Infinitiv*), Fragen durch Umstellung von Subjekt und Prädikat. Bei Kurzantworten wird nur *will* bzw. *won't* wiederholt.

Aufgepasst: Eine Form von *to do* ist bei *will* nicht möglich.

ÜBUNG 1 **An excursion**

Kate's class is going on an excursion to the seaside. Complete what Mr Benson, her English teacher, tells them before they go.

I hope/water not too cold

I think/the weather be nice

If the water isn't too cold/we go for a swim

I hope/we spend a nice day together

We/spend the afternoon there

I don't think/it rain again

Perhaps the sun/shine

I hope/you have a good time

ÜBUNG 2 Questions

a) The children have got a lot of questions. Ask their questions.

b) Imagine you are Mr Benson. What can you answer?

Jenny:
when we be there?
we need a warm pullover?
you buy us an ice cream?

Peter:
what games we play?
we be allowed to walk around on our own?

Kevin:
lunch on the beach?
play games on the beach?

Susan:
have time enough to go shopping?
when we be back?
the maths teacher come with us?

REGEL

Der Gebrauch des will-future

Das *will*-Futur gebraucht man

1. Kate will be twelve in May. All her friends will come.	1. für zukünftige Handlungen, die nicht vom persönlichen Wollen oder persönlichen Wünschen, sondern von äußeren Umständen abhängen
2. I hope the weather will be nice. Perhaps she'll have a big party, too. I think I'll go.	2. für Vorhersagen und Vermutungen und um eine Hoffnung auszudrücken. Dies ist besonders nach perhaps und Verben wie *I think, I believe, I'm sure, I hope* der Fall
3. "I must buy a present for her."– "Oh, then I'll buy her a present, too."	3. bei spontanen Entschlüssen
4. If you go to her party, I'll go, too. But I'll go only if she invites me.	4. im Hauptsatz von Bedingungssätzen und
When I see her, I'll ask her. I'll tell you when we see each other again.	im Hauptsatz von Nebensätzen der Zeit

ÜBUNG 3 Kate's hopes

Kate is looking forward to the excursion. This is what she hopes:

- lots of fun
- not rain
- weather/nice
- enough pocket money
- interesting things to see
- not too many teachers
- her friends go, too
- no homework for the next day

a) Form sentences. Begin with: She hopes, thinks, she's sure, perhaps, etc.

b) What about you? What do you hope when you go on an excursion?

ÜBUNG 4 If …

	if the coach is late?	their teacher will be angry.
	if the coach breaks down?	they will be late.
	if it rains all day?	they won't leave at 8 o'clock.
What will happen	if the sun doesn't shine?	they won't go to the beach.
	if some of the children are late?	the driver won't be happy.
	if Mr Benson is ill?	there will be no excursion.
	if Kate loses her pocket money?	they won't go for a swim.
	if they take the wrong road?	she will be unhappy.

Example: If the coach is late, they won't leave at 8 o'clock.

ÜBUNG 5 On the beach

Well, nobody is late and the bus doesn't have a breakdown. First they visit the old town, then they go to the beach. What will they do there? Here are some ideas:

When they are on the beach,

- play games
- run around
- splash[1] Mr Benson with water
- go for a swim
- have a picnic
- look for shells[2]
- play softball
- rush into the water
- be very noisy
- take off their clothes

[1]splash – bespritzen; [2]shell – Muschel

ÜBUNG 6 There are nice people ...

Before they go down to the beach, they walk around the old town and talk to each other. Complete what they say.

Kate: My bag is very heavy. There are too many things in it.
Ben: I'll carry it for you.

Jane: Look at these postcards. I need some.
Helen: ______________

Christine: I must buy something to drink.
Catherine: ______________

Susan: I can't open this bottle.
Jim: No problem. ______________

Kevin: I'm so hungry. I think I'll have a sandwich.
Ronny: Well, then, ______________

REGEL

Das *going to*-Futur

Wie du dich erinnerst, gibt es im Englischen noch ein weiteres Futur, nämlich das *going to*-Futur. Es wird mit dem Präsens von *to be* + *going to* gebildet. Dem *to* folgt ein Infinitiv. Verneinte Formen werden mit *not* gebildet, Fragen durch Umstellung von Subjekt und Prädikat.

"What are you going to do on your birthday, Kate?"
"I'm going to have a party and I'm going to invite all my friends."
"Are you going to invite Ben, too?"
"Yes, I am."
"And what about Ronny? Are you going to invite him, too?"
"No, I'm not. I'm not going to invite him."

Wenn du ausdrücken willst, dass jemand etwas in der Zukunft plant oder tun will, musst du das *going to*-Futur gebrauchen. Dies gilt vor allem dann, wenn diese Absicht schon länger bestand.

ACHTUNG

Verwechsle das *going to*-Futur nicht mit dem *present progressive*:

He's going home. (Er geht gerade nach Hause.)	He's going to go home. (Er hat vor, nach Hause zu gehen.)

ÜBUNG 7 **Plans, plans, plans ...**

Everybody has got plans, so Kate and her friends have got plans, too.

a) Complete the sentences with the going to-future.

help go invite write spend clean buy work

1. Kate's tests aren't very good, so she ________________ harder.
2. Jenny thinks that Kate's tests aren't very nice, so ____________________ .

3. Kate doesn't like Ronny, so she isn't ______________________ .

4. Helen likes Ben. She ________________________ this afternoon.

5. Linda's bike is very old. Her parents ___________________________ .

6. Betty's room is very dirty. What _______________ ? Well, she

_________________ .

7. Mary is looking forward to the holidays. She _________________ to the seaside.

8. She ____________________ her holiday there.

b) Ask Kate, Jenny, etc. about their plans.

Example: What are you going to do about your tests?
Are you going to work harder?

ÜBUNG 8 **The will- or going to-future?**

It is Kate's birthday next week. This is what she thinks.

1. If the weather is fine, we ________________ play in the garden.

2. I think everybody ________________ like that.

3. But I hope Ronny ________________ come (not). I ______________ to invite him (not).

4. There are still so many things to do. Perhaps Jenny ________________ help me.

5. Where is my shopping list? I hope Tom ________________ help me with the lemonade. I ________________ ask him when I see him.

6. And who ________________ to buy all the rest?

7. What can I do with Timmy? Well, I ________________ ask Mum if she can take him for a long, long walk. Perhaps he ________________ be tired when he gets back.

ÜBUNG 9 Plans for a party

You are planning a party. Say what you are going to do, what will or won't happen, etc. Here are some ideas. Use the *going to-* or the *will*-future. Be careful with the tenses.

- ring up my friends
- invite them
- ask them if they can come
- go to a supermarket / buy things
- ask Dad if he can help me / perhaps time to help me
- hope Mum help me, too
- make chips and sausages for us if I ask her
- hope she let us use the dining-room if it rains

ACHTUNG

Im Deutschen gebrauchen wir für zukünftige Handlungen meist nicht das Futur, sondern das Präsens. Im Englischen muss dagegen fast immer ein Futur stehen, wenn eine Handlung in der Zukunft stattfindet.

ÜBUNG 10 With a little help from your friends ...

Translate the following sentences.

1. Morgen schreiben wir einen Englisch-Test.
2. Ich hoffe, er ist nicht zu schwer.
3. Ich hoffe, meine Nachbarin hilft mir.
4. Vielleicht bekomme ich dann eine gute Note.
5. Ich frage sie heute abend, ob sie mir helfen will.
6. Wenn sie mir hilft, gebe ich ihr eine Tafel Schokolade.
7. Ich gebe sie ihr aber nur, wenn ich eine gute Note habe.
8. Wenn ich keine gute Note habe, esse ich die Tafel Schokolade selbst (= myself).

Das present perfect 14

REGEL

Die Bildung des present perfect

Wie du dich sicherlich erinnerst, wird das *present perfect* mit dem Präsens von *have (have/has)* und dem *past participle* (= Partizip der Vergangenheit) gebildet. Die Kurzformen von *have* (=*' ve/s*) sind natürlich auch möglich.

Tom hasn't finished his homework,
but his friends have already arrived.
Have they played with him yet? No, they haven't.
They haven't played with him yet.

Verneinte Formen bildest du mit *not*, Fragen durch die Umstellung von Subjekt und *has/have*. Wie bei allen zusammengesetzten Zeiten sind Formen von *to do* bei der Frage und Verneinung nicht möglich. Für die Kurzantworten gelten die üblichen Regeln.

Bei der Bildung des *past participle* musst du Folgendes beachten:

Infinitiv	**past participle**	
to finish to talk to play	he has finished she has talked they have played	finish + ed = finished: Das *past participle* bildest du normalerweise, indem du ein *-ed* an den Infinitiv anhängst.
to arrive	he has arrived	arrive + ed = arrived: Ein auslautendes *-e*, das nicht gesprochen wird, entfällt.

to stop	he has stopped	stop + ed = stopped: Bei einsilbigen Verben mit kurzem, betonten Vokal wird der auslautende Konsonant verdoppelt.
to cry	he has cried	cry + ed = cried: Nach Konsonant wird *y* zu *-i*.

Neben den regelmäßigen Formen des *past participle* gibt es – wie im Deutschen – auch unregelmäßige Formen. Diese musst du auswendig lernen.

ÜBUNG 1

The past participle

a) Form the past participle of the following verbs:

to live	lived	to give	
to carry		to play	
to say		to lie	
to show		to feel	
to catch		to think	
to bring		to tell	
to leave		to bet	
to spend		to stand	
to write		to take	

b) What's the infinitive of these participles?

paid		taught	
chosen		fallen	
lost		dropped	
thrown		tried	
fed		bought	

ÜBUNG 2 **Holiday plans**

The school year isn't over yet, but the Masons are planning their holidays. This year they want to go to the Lake District with their caravan. Have a look at the list and write down what they have already done.

Example: They have already booked a place for July.

- book a place for July
- write to the local tourist office
- buy a new road map
- have a look at it
- try to find out the best route

- begin to check their caravan
- buy a new bottle of gas
- clean the water tank
- check the tyres
- repair the rear window

ÜBUNG 3 **Preparations**

Two months later, the Masons are at the camping site where they usually have their caravan. They are preparing it for their trip to the Lake District. Mr and Mrs Mason have made a list of the things they have to do.

- wash the caravan ✔
- clean the floor
- clean the windows ✔
- make the beds
- put in some food ✔
- buy a new frying pan

- take Pete's tennis racket ✔
- buy new tennis balls
- tell the neighbours to look after the flowers ✔
- give them a key
- put in Timmy's toys ✔
- buy a new picture book

When they get home, Mrs Mason has a look at the list. She says to her husband: "Look, there are still some things to do. We have washed the caravan, but we haven't cleaned the floor yet." Go on.

ÜBUNG 4 Timmy's questions

Timmy is very excited. He wants to know what has happened to his things. Ask his questions. *Example:* Have you seen my potty?

– put my telephone in the caravan
– take away my pencils
– buy a new picture book for me
– put it in the caravan
– buy some chocolate
– pack my swimming things
– see my teddy
– find my red toy car

ÜBUNG 5 A last check

Before they leave, Mr Mason asks everybody :

"Let me see … Have we shut all the windows?" — Mrs Mason: Yes, we have.

"Have you turned off the gas, Tom?" — Tom: Yes, ______.

"Have you locked the back door, Kate?" — Kate: Yes, ______.

"Have you all been to the toilet?" — All: Yes, ______.

"Have you switched off the lights in your room?" — Tom: Yes, ______.

"Has Timmy had something to drink?" — Tom: Yes, ______.

"Have you lost your teddy again, Timmy?" — Timmy: No, ______.

"Have we forgotten anything?" — All: No, ______.

"Can we go now?" — Timmy: "No, we ______. I've left my teddy upstairs."

REGEL

Die Wortstellung beim present perfect

Have	you	washed	your hands?
Hilfsverb	**Subjekt**	**Verb**	**Objekt**
Hast	du	deine Hände	gewaschen?
		Objekt	**Verb**

Wie bei anderen zusammengesetzten Zeiten steht das Objekt im Englischen immer hinter der Verbgruppe. Von den Signalwörtern, die häufig mit dem *present perfect* gebraucht werden, stehen:

unmittelbar vor dem Verb:	never	(niemals)
	ever	(jemals)
	already	(schon)
am Satzende:	yet	(schon)
	not ... yet	(noch nicht)

Have you already packed your things?
Have you ever been late?
I have never been late.

I haven't packed my clothes yet.
Have you finished yet?

ÜBUNG 6 **Questions and answers**

Ask six questions and answer them.

Have Has	your brother you your father your sister your friends	ever already never	have be clean work go have drive sleep push play	to a caravan site? a caravan? to England? on a caravan holiday? an accident? a caravan? in a caravan? lunch in a caravan?

Example:
Have you ever driven a caravan? – No, I haven't. I've never driven a caravan.
or: – No, I haven't driven a caravan yet.

ÜBUNG 7 **Let's put it right**

Put the following sentences in their correct order.

1. everything | the Masons | packed | have | already

2. They | in the caravan | all their things | have | put

3. They | already | done | 100 kilometres | have

4. But they | not | arrived | have | yet | at their camping-site

5. not | yet | been | Timmy | sick | has

6. He is hungry now. He | not yet | has | breakfast | yet | had

7. But he | already | been | on his potty | four times | has

to be sick – sich übergeben

REGEL

Der Gebrauch des present perfect

"We have washed the caravan. It's clean now."
"Where are my car keys? I hope I haven't lost them."
"Have you seen them? Do you know where they are?"

Das *present perfect* gebraucht man für Handlungen, die zwar vorbei sind, die aber ein Ergebnis haben, das in der Gegenwart noch wirksam ist.

ÜBUNG 8 Results

What are the results? Complete the second sentence.

Example: The Masons have washed their caravan. It's clean now.

1. I have listened to you. I know what you ______________________
2. I have done my homework. Here ______________________
3. I have made my teacher angry. He ______________________
4. I have read this book. I ______________________
5. I haven't seen this film. I ______________________
6. I haven't cleaned my room yet. It ______________________

ÜBUNG 9 What has happened?

Can you finish these sentences?

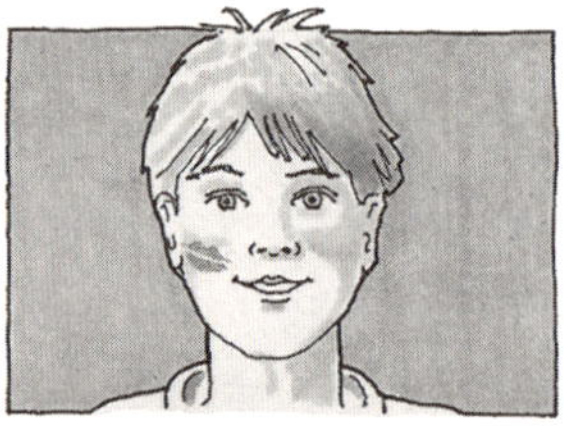

There's lipstick on Tom's face. (Jenny – kiss him goodbye)

Here are Mr Mason's car keys. (find again)

Here is Timmy's potty. (Timmy – put it in the fridge)

Here are the Masons in front of their caravan. They are ready to leave. (pack everything)

Look at that window. It's not shut. (somebody forget to shut it)

That's the street where the Masons live. It's empty now. (The Masons – leave)

Example: There's lipstick on Tom's face. Jenny has kissed him goodbye.

15 Das simple past

REGEL

Die Bildung des simple past

The children are back at school. They are talking about the things that they did in their holidays:

Mike:
We visited the Isle of Wight and did quite a lot of things there. I even tried to talk to some Germans there, but they just laughed when I tried to say something in German to them. I think my German sounded a bit funny to them. So I stopped speaking German to them and laughed at their English.

Tom:
We went to the Lake District. We found a fantastic camping site and had a great time there. Only Timmy had a bad time. One day he ... but I'll tell you about that later.

Jenny:
I was in London. I stayed there with my aunt and my uncle. They were very strict and never let me go out alone. It's too dangerous for girls like you, they said.

Bei den regelmäßigen Formen wird das *simple past* wie das *past participle* mit dem Infinitiv + *ed* gebildet. Beachte dabei die folgenden Regeln:

1. Bei Verben, die auf ein nicht gesprochenes -*e* enden, fällt ein *e* aus:
cycle + ed = cycled

2. Nach Konsonant + *y* wird das *y* zu *i*. Nach Vokal bleibt das *y* erhalten (vgl. auch die Pluralbildung und die 3. Person Singular im *simple present*).

try + ed	= tried
stay + ed	= stayed

3. Einsilbige Verben mit kurzem, betontem Vokal, die auf Konsonant enden, verdoppeln den letzten Konsonant:

stop + ed	= stopped

Unregelmäßige Formen

Wie im Deutschen gibt es auch im Englischen unregelmäßige Formen, die du einfach lernen musst. Einige findest du oben im Text.

Die Formen des *simple past* sind für alle Personen gleich. Dies gilt sowohl für die regelmäßigen wie die unregelmäßigen Formen. Im Übrigen: Ein *-s* in der dritten Person Singular gibt es nur im *simple present* und bei den Formen von *to be*.

Das *simple past* von *to be*

Auch die Formen von *to be* sind unregelmäßig. Sie lauten:

I	was	we	were
you	were	you	were
he, she, it	was	they	were

ÜBUNG 1 **Mind the spelling and the pronunciation**

Mark the regular and irregular verbs with different colours.

say buy stop sit lead write read tear play cry catch swim set ride hear carry think meet feed hide fly teach let bring lose get hit break

ÜBUNG 2 The Masons leave

Put in the missing verbs. Use the simple past.

know want arrive be leave carry see
come see go run hear get shut

The Masons ______________ to leave early, but as usual it ______________ quite late when they ______________ off. Kate ______________ still tired and Tom ______________ to finish a letter. Then Timmy's potty ______________ missing and nobody ______________ where it ______________ . When they ______________ all in the car again, somebody ______________ that a window ______________ still open. So Mr Mason ______________ out of the car, ______________ into the house again and ______________ it. When he ______________ back, Timmy ______________ to go to the toilet again. So Mr Mason ______________ out of the car again and ______________ Timmy to the bathroom. When they______________ back, they ______________ the telephone ringing. So Tom ______________ out of the car and ______________ into the house again. But he ______________ not fast enough. When he ______________ , the line ______________ dead. But finally they ______________ ready to leave.

ÜBUNG 3 The Masons' trip

Retell the Masons' trip to their camping site. Use the simple past.

finally leave at 11 o'clock	first stop at 11.30/ Timmy sick[1]	second stop at 12.15/Timmy sick again	lunch at 1 p.m./ when leave/forget Timmy's teddy
get in car at 2 p.m./drive on	Mr Mason take a short cut/ lose two hours	arrive at 6 p.m. at the camping site/ try to put up tent[2] for Tom/tent collapse[3]	have supper at 8/ go to bed at 9/ all very tired

[1]to be sick – sich übergeben [2]a tent – Zelt [3]to collapse – zusammenbrechen

REGEL

Verneinte Formen

Timmy	did not (= didn't)	enjoy	the trip.
He	did not (= didn't)	feel	fine.
Subjekt +	***did not (= didn't)* +**	**Infinitiv**	

Timmy	was not (= wasn't)	happy.
Tom and Kate	were not (= weren't)	sick.
Subjekt +	***was/were not***	

Vollverben werden im *simple past* mit *did not* bzw. *didn't* verneint. Danach steht immer der Infinitiv.

Was/were werden mit *not* verneint. Statt *was not/were not* sind auch die entsprechenden Kurzformen *(wasn't/weren't)* möglich.

ÜBUNG 4 **The first night**

Write out these sentences. Use negative forms.

The first night Timmy not sleep very well – not have his teddy – not quiet enough at the camping site – at home not sleep in the same bed with Kate – his sister not leave him enough room – she not want him in "her" bed – Timmy not warm enough – not have nice dreams – not happy that night.

ÜBUNG 5 **The first day**

Write down what they did the first day.

Example: The first day they didn't get up early. They had a late breakfast.

	not cook in the caravan	write a letter to Jenny.
Timmy	not sick any more	have a late breakfast
Tom	not do any work	go for a walk
Kate	not get up early	buy a new teddy for Timmy
Mr Mason	not do any homework	have lunch in a restaurant
Mrs Mason	not lie on the beach	look for new friends
	not stay in the caravan	feel better
	not feel tired any more	walk around the camping site

REGEL

Fragen und Kurzantworten

Did	you have a nice holiday?	Yes, I did.
Didn't	you go swimming?	No, I didn't.

Wenn du eine Frage im *simple past* mit Vollverben bilden willst, musst du *did* bzw. *didn't* gebrauchen. Danach steht immer ein Infinitiv. In Kurzantworten wird das Vollverb durch *did* bzw. *didn't* ersetzt.

Were	you	on the beach?	No, I wasn't.
Was	the water	cold?	Yes, it was.
Weren't	you	unhappy?	No, I wasn't.

Bei *to be* darfst du keine Form von *to do* gebrauchen. Du bildest die Frage allein durch Umstellung von Subjekt und Prädikat. Bei Kurzantworten stehen die entsprechenden Formen von *to be*.

ÜBUNG 6 **Questions**

When Tom was back from his holidays, his friends asked him a lot of questions. Complete the questions and give short answers.

1. ______________ you go to the Lake District for the first time? (Yes)
2. ______________ you like it there? (Yes)
3. ______________ you sleep in a tent? (Yes)
4. ______________ it cold at night? (No)
5. ______________ you go swimming? (Yes)
6. ______________ you make any friends? (Yes)
7. ______________ there any other girls? (Yes)
8. ______________ you like them? (No)
9. ______________ they nicer than Jenny? (No)
10. ______________ they older than you? (Yes)

REGEL

Fragen mit Fragewörtern

a) nach dem Subjekt		b) nach allen anderen Satzteilen			
Who	was on the beach?	Where	was	Timmy?	
What	happened?	What	did	he	do there?
Who	didn't come back?	Why	didn't	he	come back?
Who	broke his arm?	What	did	he	break?

Auch bei Ergänzungsfragen, d. h. Fragen mit Fragewörtern, musst du *did* oder *didn't* gebrauchen. Bei Fragen nach dem Subjekt ist *didn't* dagegen nur in verneinten Fragen möglich. Bei Fragen mit *to be* steht nie ein *did*!

ÜBUNG 7

Tom's letter

Dear Mike,

Something terrible happened yesterday. I wanted to go to the beach with Timmy and Kate. Timmy had his teddy and his picture book in his hands, so perhaps he didn't see where he was going. Anyway – suddenly Timmy stumbled* and fell over a big stone. I turned round and saw that it was Timmy. He still had his teddy in his right hand; but his arm looked strange. Timmy didn't cry at first, but his face looked very white. I didn't know what to do, so I told Kate to run home and to fetch Mum or Dad. Kate did what I told her and five minutes later Mum and Dad were there. They carried Timmy back to the caravan and phoned a doctor. When she came, she examined Timmy ...

When Mr and Mrs Mason saw Kate, they knew that something had happened. Imagine what they asked Kate.

*to stumble – stolpern

ÜBUNG 8 At the hospital

Well, Timmy had to go to hospital. A doctor examined him again. Ask the doctor's questions. Here are some ideas to help you.

Example: Did it hurt, Timmy?

– hurt?	– fall on your arm?	– your teddy all right?
– how?	– cry?	– who help you?
– why?	– when?	– anybody with you?

REGEL

Die Vergangenheit von einigen Hilfsverben

When the doctor examined Timmy, he found out that Timmy's arm was broken.

So Timmy couldn't go home.
His parents couldn't take him home.
But they could come and talk to him.

His parents were allowed to visit him.
He was not allowed to get up the first day.
But he was allowed to get up the next day.

He had to stay in hospital for some days.
Did he have to stay in bed all the time? No, he didn't.
He didn't have to stay in bed all the time.

Von den englischen Hilfsverben hat nur *can* (= können) eine Vergangenheitsform *(could/could not* bzw. die Kurzform *couldn't* = konnte/konnte nicht). Für die anderen Hilfsverben musst du Ersatzverben (= so genannte *substitutes*) verwenden und zwar für:

may	dürfen	was/were allowed to	durfte
may not/ mustn't	nicht dürfen	wasn't/weren't allowed to	durfte nicht
must	müssen	had to	musste
needn't	nicht müssen/ nicht brauchen	didn't have to	musste nicht/ brauchte nicht

Nach Hilfsverben und Ersatzverben steht immer ein Infinitiv. Bei Hilfsverben steht jedoch – im Unterschied zu Ersatzverben – kein *to* vor dem Infinitiv.

ÜBUNG 9

At the hospital

The first day after his operation there were some things Timmy was not allowed to do or couldn't do. What could he do? What was he allowed to do? What did he have to do?

– play with his teddy

– draw pictures with his right arm

– talk to the nurses

– run around in the room

– make his bed

– look at his picture book

– be careful with his arm

– keep his arm still (= ruhig)

– play in the corridor

– clean the room

– stay in bed all day

– eat his meals

ÜBUNG 10

Questions

Now ask Timmy what he had to do and what he was allowed to do.

Example: Did you have to stay in bed all the time? – No, I didn't.

DIKTATE 10 11

Und jetzt solltest du als Abschluss dieses Kapitels zwei Diktate schreiben. Lass dir den ersten Text diktieren: Diktat Nr. 10.

In diesem Diktat kommt ein Wort vor, das du vielleicht noch nicht kennst:

boat [bəut] = Boot; Schiff

Mit dem zweiten Diktat kannst du das *simple past* von unregelmäßigen Verben üben: Diktat Nr. 11.

Auch in diesem Diktat kommen zwei Wörter vor, die du vielleicht noch nicht kennst:

open day = Tag der offenen Tür
pond [pɒnd] = Teich

Das simple past und das past progressive im Vergleich

16

REGEL

Der Gebrauch des simple past

Mr Mason had an accident, too. But it was many years ago. When did he have the accident? It was in 1975, when he was much younger than today.

1. Das *simple past* steht bei Handlungen, die in der Vergangenheit stattfanden und abgeschlossen sind. Es findet sich nach Signalwörtern wie *yesterday, a week (a month, year) ago, last Friday (month), in 1995*. Oft steht es auch nach *when*.

He played in a football team then. They played every Saturday. His team wasn't a good team, so they often lost. But sometimes they also won.

2. Es steht bei wiederholten und gewohnheitsmäßigen Handlungen, die in der Vergangenheit stattfanden. Signalwörter sind hier – wie schon beim *simple present* – *always, usually, often, sometimes,* etc.

He remembered one match: They were on their way home when their bus suddenly ran off the road. He felt a pain in his left leg, and things went black before his eyes. Then he didn't feel anything else. Afterwards, they told him that his left leg was broken.

3. Das *simple past* wird verwendet für abgeschlossene, aufeinander folgende Handlungen der Vergangenheit. Signalwörter sind hier *first, then, after that, the next moment, the next morning, last night, when, suddenly,* etc.

ÜBUNG 1

What happened after the accident?

Tell Timmy's story. Use first, then, after that, so, when, etc. to connect the sentences.

Tom send Kate back to parents	Kate run to caravan	Kate tell parents all about Timmy's accident	Mrs Mason phone a doctor
doctor arrive/ examine Timmy	call an ambulance	ambulance arrive/ the ambulance men put Timmy on a stretcher*	drive him to the hospital

*stretcher – Bahre

REGEL

Das past progressive

What were the Masons doing when Timmy had his accident?
Were they going to the beach, too? No, they weren't.

Mr Mason was talking to a neighbour.
They were having a coke and talking about football.
Mrs Mason was reading a book.
She wasn't listening to what they were talking about.

Das *past progressive* wird mit *was/were* und dem *present participle* gebildet. Bei Fragen wird umgestellt (Hilfsverb – Subjekt – Verb); verneinte Formen werden mit *not* gebildet. *To do* ist bei Fragen und bei der Verneinung nicht möglich. Zur Bildung des *present participle* vergleiche Kapitel 8.

ACHTUNG

Nicht alle Verben können im Englischen eine *progressive form* bilden. Verben wie *to be, to belong, to see, to feel, to hear, to want, to like, to know, to think, to sound* u. a. haben im Englischen meist keine *progressive form*. Hier musst du die *simple forms* gebrauchen.

ÜBUNG 2

What people were doing

When Timmy had his accident, a lot of people were on the beach. Say what they were doing.

– a woman reading a magazine
– a man lying in a deckchair
– some people swimming
– two children playing with a ball
– a girl putting on her clothes
– a boy listening to a radio
– a family having a picnic

ÜBUNG 3

Asking people

You are the reporter of the local newspaper. You want to find out what people were doing when Timmy had his accident. So you ask them.

Example: What were you doing when the accident happened?
Were you having a swim?

Go on.

REGEL

Das *simple past* und das *past progressive*

Neu einsetzende oder neue Handlungen: *simple past*

When the ambulance arrived,

Gleichzeitigkeit mit neuer Handlung: *past progressive*

Timmy was still lying on the beach. He was crying. A lot of people were standing around him.

Was geschah dann? (neue Handlung)

The ambulance men examined Timmy. Then they put him on a stretcher and drove him off to hospital.

Und dann? (neue Handlung)

When the ambulance left,

Was passierte gerade zu dieser Zeit?

the people were still standing there.

Wie du bereits weißt, steht das *simple past* für Handlungen, die vorüber sind und einander folgen. Solche Handlungsketten kommen vor allem in Erzählungen und Berichten vor. Hier liegt auch der Grund dafür, warum du das *simple past* in einer Geschichte oder einem Bericht für jede neu einsetzende Handlung verwenden musst.

Im Unterschied zum *simple past* musst du das *past progressive* für Handlungen verwenden, die zu dem Zeitpunkt noch nicht vorüber waren, als eine neue Handlung eintrat. Handlungen im *past progressive* bilden daher sozusagen den Hintergrund für neu einsetzende Handlungen. Ein häufiges Signalwort für eine solche Hintergrundshandlung ist hier *while*.

Im Deutschen steht für das *past progressive* oft „gerade".

Vergleiche: Tom was talking to Kate when Timmy fell over.
(... redete gerade)

ÜBUNG 4

Your idea

The Masons had one neighbour who didn't like them. So he told people a lot of bad things about them.

When poor Timmy broke his arm,	Mr Mason his wife nobody Kate Tom	just get up drink beer with their neighbours look after Timmy lie in the sun smoke and talk still lie in bed write a letter just have breakfast

Write six sentences.

ÜBUNG 5

At the hospital

Tell the story. Use the correct tenses.

1. While they (sit) in the waiting-room/ the door (open). A man (come) in.
2. He (wear) a bandage round his head.
3. He (say) good morning/then he (sit) down/(look) for a newspaper.
4. He (open) newspaper/ (begin) to read.
5. While (read) his newspaper, a nurse (come) in.
6. She (tell) Mr Mason and Mrs Mason to follow her.
7. She (lead) them to the room where Timmy (wait).
8. There a doctor (talk) to Timmy.
9. Timmy (ask) him a lot of questi-ons.
10. When the doctor (see) them/(call) them to Timmy's bed.
11. Timmy (laugh). He (be) happy he (can) go home.
12. They (thank) the doctor/(pack) Timmy's things. Then they (leave) the hospital.

ÜBUNG 6

In the waiting-room

A few days later, the Masons were allowed to take Timmy home. But they had to wait until Timmy was ready. There were a lot of patients in the waiting-room who had to wait for the doctor, too. Why were they waiting for the doctor?

play football/
fall to the ground/
broke my arm

climb a rock/
slip

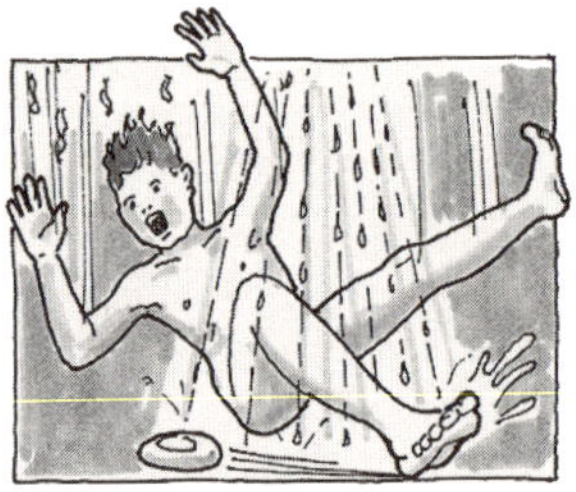

I slip/have a shower/
broke three ribs*

*rib – Rippe

I clean the windows/
ladder break/
fall onto the floor

I lie in my deckchair/
it collapse

I do my homework/
fall asleep/
fall off the chair

ÜBUNG 7

A ghost story

The simple past or the past progressive?

Timmy still ______________ (have) to be very careful with his arm and he ______________ (can't) go for a swim, of course. So everybody ______________ (have) to keep him busy. Tom often ______________ (read) ghost stories to him. Timmy's favourite story ______________ (be) about an American family who ______________ (want) to buy an old castle in England. When they ______________ (come) to the castle, the sun ______________ (not shine). It ______________ (rain) and thunder ______________ (sound) again and again. When they ______________ (enter) the castle, a flash of lightning[1] ______________ (fill) the hall and there ______________ (be) lightning and thunder all through the night. The next morning when they ________________ (come) down, they ________________ (see) blood[2] on the floor. The next night they ______________ (hear) strange noises in the corridor outside their bedrooms. When Mr Otis ______________ (open) the door, he ______________ (see) a terrible old man. Long hair ______________ (fall) from his head, his eyes ______________ (be) likc fire and he …

[1]lightning – Blitz
[2]blood – Blut

17 Das simple past und present perfect im Vergleich

REGEL

Zum Gebrauch des present perfect und des simple past

present perfect	simple past
für Handlungen, die zwar vorbei sind, aber in der Gegenwart noch Folgen haben:	für Handlungen, die abgeschlossen und daher vorüber sind:
The Masons have packed everything. They have turned off the gas. They have already locked the door. They have paid for the camping site, too.	They packed yesterday. They turned the gas off after breakfast. When did they lock the door? They paid ten weeks ago.
Das *present perfect* betont das gegenwärtige Ergebnis. Es steht daher meist ohne eine Zeitangabe der Vergangenheit. Mit dem *present perfect* gebrauchte Signalwörter sind: *already, yet, not ... yet, never, ever,* etc.	Das *simple past* betont, dass Handlungen vorbei sind. Es steht daher oft mit Zeitangaben der Vergangenheit wie *ago, yesterday, at that time, last week, in 1983;* häufig auch bei *when.* Bei allen diesen Zeitangaben der Vergangenheit muss unbedingt das *simple past* stehen!

ÜBUNG 1 Back at school

All the children are back at school. They ask each other lots of questions. Complete these questions. Put in the simple past or the present perfect.

1. When __________ you __________ (come) back?
2. Where __________ you __________ (go?)
3. __________ you __________ (like) your stay there?
4. __________ ever __________ (be) to Italy?
5. __________ you __________ (do) anything for school as Old Misery __________ (tell) you?
6. __________ you __________ (play) tennis in the holidays?
7. How many postcards __________ you __________ (write)?
8. Where __________ you __________ (buy) these shoes?
9. What __________ (be) the weather like? __________ it __________ (rain) a lot?
10. __________ you already__________ (see) Mike? Is he late again?

ÜBUNG 2 Your answers

Can you answer the questions in exercise 1?

ÜBUNG 3 Mike's photos

During the holidays Mike took a lot of photos. He is showing them to Tom and Jenny. Complete the sentences and put in the correct tenses (simple present, simple past, present perfect).

Look! This is our hotel/stay there for two weeks

That is the beach in front of our hotel/ always go swimming there

This is our car/ accident/we not repair it yet

This is Carisbrooke Castle/visit the castle/ you know/that Charles be a prisoner here?

That is Tim/I play with him a lot/we often go to the beach/have a swim together

And that girl is his sister/we play with her sometimes

ÜBUNG 4

Mike's "new life"

Mike's last school report wasn't very good, so during the holidays he made plans to begin a "new life". He made a list of the things he wanted to do. After three weeks at school he had a look at the list again and added two or three things to it. Then he read it to himself.

Example: I haven't been late any more. I was only late the first day.

Go on.

be late any more (only the first day)
listen to my teachers (nearly always!)
not play during lessons (never again)
talk to my neighbour (only sometimes)
not forget my books again (only yesterday)
do my homework in all subjects (only not do it last Monday)
go home immediately after school (usually)
write better tests (got good marks!)
learn more German (spend nearly ten minutes on my German homework yesterday!)
not watch so much TV (yesterday only one hour!)

REGEL

Der deutsche und englische Gebrauch des present perfect

Das Perfekt im Deutschen
„... gestern sind wir heimgekommen; wir haben unser Gepäck aus dem Auto geholt und haben dann zu Abend gegessen. Dann sind wir ins Bett gegangen und sind sofort eingeschlafen."

In der deutschen Umgangssprache gebraucht man das Perfekt vor allem dazu, eine Geschichte zu erzählen oder über etwas zu berichten. Dies ist im Englischen nicht möglich.

Das *simple past* im Englischen
"... yesterday we came home; we fetched our luggage from the car; then we had supper. After that we went to bed and fell asleep immediately."

Wenn man im Englischen etwas erzählen oder berichten will, gebraucht man das *simple past*. Es ist die eigentliche Erzählzeit im Englischen und findet sich vor allem nach Signalwörtern wie *first, then, after that, at that moment, suddenly* etc.

ÜBUNG 5

The first lesson

As you know, Tom and his class have German, too. In the first lesson after the holidays they had to tell old Old Misery, their German teacher, about their holidays. They had to do it in German. This is what they told him. Can you put in English what they said?

Wir sind gestern zurückgekommen.

Ich bin oft schwimmen gegangen.

Ich habe einen deutschen Jungen kennen gelernt.

Ich habe Mike in den Ferien getroffen.

Ich habe sehr viel Deutsch gesprochen

Wir haben einen Unfall gehabt.

Ich habe keine Hausaufgaben in den Ferien gemacht.

Ich bin richtig fett geworden.

Ich habe in den Ferien zu viel gegessen.

Wir haben uns in den Ferien viele Schlösser angeschaut.

ÜBUNG 6 A ghost story

In one of the first lessons Tom's class had to write about a holiday adventure. These are Mike's notes for his story. Can you write it out? Be careful with the tenses!

In the holidays we visit Carisbrooke Castle – old castle – famous, too, because Charles be a prisoner there some hundred years ago, before his execution. People say – he not found peace yet – his ghost still walk there.

When we get there, the sky very dark – when walk through the entrance – begin to rain – so go into the castle – very dark in there, too; lots of strange noises suddenly a door open – when I look there – I see something green – come towards me – ran out of the building and tell everything to my parents – not believe me – just laugh at me.

Two days after the holidays over – we must go home again – That night I go to bed early, but wake up at midnight – strange noise – see something green – it sit at my desk – before I can say anything, it gone – soon forget this, but two weeks later I wake up again – see a green shadow at my desk again – it write something in an exercise book – I very afraid, not move – five minutes later it gone. As it not come back, I get up – go to the desk – there see my German exercise book – open – a note in the book: Don't do any homework tomorrow or you'll die! This is what the ghost tell me – that's why I not do any homework last Tuesday.

ÜBUNG 7

So sorry, but ...

Not all pupils like homework. Here is a list of things you can say when you have forgotten it. Use the correct tenses.

I couldn't do my homework I can't show you my homework	B E C A U S E	my neighbour (be) ill. I (not remember) where I (put) it. I (leave) my book at school. I (leave) it on the bus/at home. my mother father/sister (be) ill yesterday. I (feel) so ill in the afternoon. my pen (not work). I (forget) my schoolbag. my baby brother/baby sister (eat) it. my exercise book (be) full. my baby brother (make) a plane out of it. I (must) repair my bike. my mother (not have) time to do it.

18 Adjektive

REGEL

Der Gebrauch der Adjektive

What do you think? Are there any nice and clever girls/boys in your class? Or are they all silly and stupid?

Adjektive beziehen sich immer auf Substantive oder Pronomen. Dabei geben sie Eigenschaften der jeweiligen Sachen oder Personen an.

Wie im Deutschen steht das Adjektiv meist unmittelbar vor dem Substantiv *(a nice boy)*; nach bestimmten Verben wie *to be* steht es auch nach dem Substantiv:
Tom is nice.

ÜBUNG 1

What's your English teacher, friend, brother, sister like?

Choose three adjectives for each person.

Example: What's your English teacher like?
Let me see – she is clever and intelligent, but she can be strange, too.

beautiful bad good boring busy careful crazy

exciting fantastic noisy fat loud modern poor

quick slow strange tall small thin strong

worried intelligent dangerous funny powerful

interesting wonderful clever difficult heavy nice

ÜBUNG 2 What you think

Choose at least three adjectives from the list in exercise 1 to show what you think about

comics English tests boys TV teachers

books baby brothers/sisters

pop music films girls football

Example: Girls are nice, clever and intelligent.

ÜBUNG 3 What's the opposite?

Example: A good teacher – a bad teacher

a funny girl ________________	a clever pupil ________________
an old town ________________	a quiet boy ________________
a small boy ________________	a happy child ________________
a good mark ________________	a difficult text ________________
a boring film ________________	a silly person ________________
a fast runner ________________	a terrible story ________________
a bad driver ________________	a rich man ________________

REGEL

Die Steigerung der Adjektive

Adjektive werden im Englischen folgendermaßen gesteigert:

	Positiv	Komparativ	Superlativ
einsilbige Adjektive	poor	poorer	the poorest
	fine	finer	the finest
	big	bigger	the biggest

zweisilbige Adjektive auf *-y* und *-er*	funny	funnier	the funniest
	angry	angrier	the angriest
	clever	cleverer	the cleverest
die meisten anderen zweisilbigen Adjektive sowie alle Adjektive mit drei und mehr Silben	famous	more famous	the most famous
	terrible	more terrible	the most terrible
	difficult	more difficult	the most difficult

Der Vergleich im Satz

Die verschiedenen Formen der Adjektive benutzt man dazu, Vergleiche zu ziehen. Gleichheit bzw. Ungleichheit werden folgendermaßen ausgedrückt:

	Gleichheit:	
Mike is as tall as Tom.	... (eben)so ... wie ...	as + Positiv + as
Is he also as intelligent?	... (eben)so ...	
	Ungleichheit:	
Tom's sister isn't as tall as Mike.	... nicht so ... wie ...	not as + Pos. + as
She is smaller than Mike.	... kleiner als ...	Komparativ + than
But she is more intelligent than Mike.	... intelligenter als ...	

Vor und nach der Grundform des Adjektivs steht immer *as,* nach dem Komparativ dagegen immer *than.*

Verwechsle *than* (= als) nicht mit *then* (= dann, damals).

ACHTUNG

1. Adjektive mit einer Silbe und zweisilbige Adjektive auf *-y* und *-er* bilden den Komparativ mit *-er* und den Superlativ mit *-est.* Dabei entfällt ein auslautendes *-e.*
2. Einsilbige Adjektive mit einem kurzen, betonten Vokal, die auf Konsonant enden, verdoppeln den auslautenden Konsonanten.
3. Zweisilbige Adjektive, die nicht auf *-y* und *-er* enden, sowie alle Adjektive, die mehr als zwei Silben haben, bilden den Komparativ mit *more* und den Superlativ mit *most.*

Die folgenden Adjektive haben unregelmäßige Steigerungsformen:
good – better – the best   bad – worse – the worst

ÜBUNG 4

Comparatives and superlatives

Form the comparatives and superlatives of the following adjectives:

good, careful, noisy, fat, powerful, nice, intelligent, heavy, dangerous, quick

ÜBUNG 5

Tom's family

Compare the persons in the picture. Use the superlatives and comparatives of tall and small.

Dad 1.85 cm Mum 1.70 cm Grandfather 1.80 cm Grandmother 1.65 cm

Tom 1.52 cm Kate 1.40 cm Timmy 0.92 cm

ÜBUNG 6

Comparisons

Susan and Betty, two girls in Tom's class, don't like each other. So their ideas are often different.

Example: Susan: I think football is more exciting than volleyball.
Betty: No, it isn't, but it's more dangerous.
Susan: More dangerous? I think volleyball is as dangerous as football.

tennis	difficult	English	nice	comics	funny
swimming	expensive	German	useful	books	interesting

ÜBUNG 7 What girls whisper

Susan and Jane are talking about Mike, the new boy in class. Can you complete what they say?Use the following adjectives: tall, strong, silly, bad, good, nice in their different forms.

Susan: He is very tall. I think he is ________ boy in our class.

Jane: Is he? No, I think David is ________ him.

Susan: And he's so strong. He must be ________ boy in our class.

Jane: He is very nice. I think he is even ________ than Tom.

Susan: Look at his hair. It has got the same colour ________ your hair. Have you got the same shoes, too?

Jane: Oh, don't be stupid; or you'll get a prize for ________ questions.

Susan: Is he good at maths? Do you think he can help me? I need somebody who is ________ Tom. You know, at maths Tom is even ________ me.

Jane: Why don't you go and ask him? He looks a bit silly, but perhaps he is ________ at maths ________ he looks.

Susan: Have you seen any of his photos? Anne told me his photos are ________ photos she has ever seen.

ÜBUNG 8

Questions – questions

You have already done a lot of exercises now. Can you answer some questions?

1. Has your English become ______________________ (good)?
2. Let's hope it hasn't become ______________________ (bad).
3. Is the number of mistakes in your English tests ______________________ or ______________________ (big/small) now?
4. Were the exercises very ______________________ (boring)?
5. Were they ______________________ (interesting) than in your textbook?
6. Were they ______________________ (boring) as in your textbook?
7. Or were they ______________________ (bad)?
8. Was the grammar ______________________ (clear) enough?
9. Or was the grammar in your textbook ______________________ (easy)?
10. We hope that you didn't find things too ______________________ (difficult).

DIKTAT 12

Und jetzt solltest du als Abschluss dieses Kapitels ein kurzes Diktat schreiben. Lass dir den Text diktieren: Diktat Nr. 12. Achte besonders auf die richtige Schreibweise von „then" und „than"!

19 Adverbien

REGEL

Adverbien der Art und Weise

Wenn du sagen willst, wie man etwas tut – ob schnell, langsam, gründlich etc. –, gebrauchst du ein Adverb und zwar ein Adverb der Art und Weise. Solche Adverbien gibt es auch im Englischen (so genannte *adverbs of manner*).

Ein Hauptproblem dieser Adverbien ist, dass sie im Deutschen oft die gleiche Form wie das entsprechende Adjektiv haben. Vergleiche:

adverb	**adjective**
Er singt schön.	Seine Stimme ist schön.

Im Englischen musst du jedoch zwischen zwei verschiedenen Formen unterscheiden:

He sings beautifully.	His voice is beautiful.

Du bildest diese Adverbien, indem du an das Adjektiv ein *-ly* anhängst:

bad + ly	badly
careful + ly	carefully
nice + ly	nicely

ACHTUNG

Beachte jedoch dabei:

1. Bei Adjektiven, die auf Konsonant + *y* enden, wird das *y* zu *i:*
   happy + ly happily
   noisy + ly noisily

2. Adjektive, die auf *-ble* enden, verlieren das *-le:*
   terrible + ly terribly

3. *Good, hard, fast* haben unregelmäßige Adverbformen:
   Tom is a good singer. He sings well.
   Mike is a fast runner. He runs fast.
   Jenny is a hard worker. She works hard.

ÜBUNG 1 Tom's class

Add the missing adverbs.

1. Betty is a good dancer. She dances ______________
2. Kevin is a fast runner. He runs ____________________
3. Ann has a beautiful voice. She sings ______________________
4. Susan is a quiet girl. She does everything _______________
5. Jim is a very noisy boy. He always runs around ___________________
6. Barbara is a hard worker. She works ____________________
7. Kate is a clever girl. She always answers _____________________
8. John is a happy boy. He always laughs ___________________
9. Jane is a terrible dancer. She dances _____________________
10. Matthew is very good at German. He speaks German very _____________

ÜBUNG 2 **What can you do, your friends do?**

First say what you can do, then make up a portrait of a friend or pupil of your class. Use adverbs and adjectives.

Example: a) I am good at English. I can speak English very well.
b) My friend ...

noisy	fast	hard	easy	careful
slow	clever	intelligent	bad	excellent
quick	nice	boring	exciting	wonderful

REGEL

Adjektiv oder Adverb?

Als Grundregeln solltest du dir merken:

1. Wie du bereits weißt, beziehen sich Adjektive immer auf Pronomen oder Substantive. Vor einem Substantiv steht daher immer ein Adjektiv und nie ein Adverb:

   He is a careful worker.
   He is a dangerous driver.

   Adverbien der Art und Weise geben an, wie etwas getan wird. Sie beziehen sich daher immer auf ein Verb:

   He works carefully.
   He drives dangerously.

2. Ist *to be* das Verb eines Satzes, steht immer ein Adjektiv.

   She is clever and intelligent.

   Ein Adverb steht dagegen, wenn *to be* Teil einer *progressive form* ist.

   She is answering intelligently.

ÜBUNG 3 A fire at school

Adjective or adverb? Put in the correct forms.

All the children were __________ (quiet) sitting in the classroom when suddenly they heard a siren. What was it? Could it be one of those __________ (silly) fire alarms? Then they all saw it. Smoke was coming out in __________ (thick) clouds from the main building and in one room they saw ______ (red) flames. They were all very ______________ (excited) and immediately wanted to leave the classroom. "Be ____________ (quiet)", the teacher shouted __________ (angry). "You needn't be _________ (afraid). Remember what you must do when there is a fire alarm. You Pete, you get up ____________ (quick) and shut these windows. Then let's leave the room, but don't run. Let's leave it __________ (slow) and in __________ (good) order. Keep together and remember to shut the door ____________ (careful). Leave your things in the room if you can't pack them ________ (quick). Are you all __________ (ready) ? So let's get out ____________ (slow) now. Jane, don't forget the register. Jimmy, you are the last; be ______________ (sure) to shut the door behind you."

ÜBUNG 4 Chaos at school

Add the missing adjectives or adverbs.

When they came into the corridor, there were a lot of things their teacher didn't like.

1. Lots of windows and doors were still __________ (open).
2. Some pupils were running around __________ (excited) in the corridor.
3. Others were still ________________ (quiet) packing their things.
4. One pupil was ___________ (busy) copying his homework from his friend's exercise-book. He wasn't even writing very ________ (fast).
5. Another pupil was reading a comic. He didn't think it was ____________ (dangerous) to remain in the building.

6. Some were ______________ (excited) watching the smoke from the windows of their classrooms.
7. Others were ______________ (happy) that there was a fire at their school.
8. A ______________ (good) fire is less ________________ (boring) than an English lesson, one of them said ______________ (excited).
9. And there will be no English tomorrow, somebody else added __________ (quick).

ÜBUNG 5

Giving orders

What do you think the teacher told them? Give orders; use adverbs or adverbs in your orders.

Example: Be quiet now and shut the windows quickly.
Go on.

REGEL

Die Stellung der Adverbien der Art und Weise

They talked quickly. He listened excitedly. He smiled happily.	Adverbien der Art und Weise stehen nach dem Verb, wenn kein Objekt vorhanden ist.
They left the room quietly. They shut the door quickly.	Ist ein direktes Objekt vorhanden, so steht das Adverb zumeist nach diesem Objekt.
They quietly left the room.	Ist das Adverb weniger betont, kann es in diesem Fall auch vor dem Verb stehen.

Aufgepasst: Im Unterschied zum Deutschen darfst du im Englischen nie ein Adverb zwischen das Verb und das direkte Objekt setzen!

Zur Stellung der Adverbien der Häufigkeit siehe das folgende Kapitel.

ÜBUNG 6

Helping hands ...

Put the adverbs in their correct place.

Very soon they heard another noise. It was the siren of a big fire-engine that came into the school yard. And this is what they heard and saw:

angry quick careful nervous
worried busy fast excited

1. "Get out of our way", one man shouted.
2. Four men jumped out of it.
3. Two of them ran into the building.
4. They raised a ladder.
5. One man climbed up the ladder.
6. Another man fetched the water hose.
7. "Is there anybody injured?", another man asked.
8. "Where can we take the water from?", one man asked.
9. "What are we waiting for?", another shouted.
10. "Where do we begin?", one man asked.

DIKTAT 13

Und jetzt solltest du als Abschluss dieses Kapitels ein kurzes Diktat schreiben. Lass dir den Text diktieren: Diktat Nr. 13.

20 Die Wortstellung im Englischen

REGEL

Die Stellung des Subjekts im Aussagesatz

Da englische Substantive außer der Pluralendung keine Endungen haben, liegt die Wortstellung im Englischen fest. Du kannst daher die Wortstellung nicht einfach ändern, ohne dass sich auch der Sinn des Satzes ändert. Vergleiche:

The dog	bites	the postman.	Der Hund beißt den Briefträger. (= Objekt).
The postman	bites	the dog.	Der Briefträger (= Subjekt) beißt den Hund.

Wie du aus diesem Beispiel siehst, bestimmt im Englischen die Wortstellung die Funktion eines Substantivs (oder Pronomens): Steht es in einem Aussagesatz vor dem Verb, ist es Subjekt. Steht es nach dem Verb, ist es Objekt des Aussagesatzes. Aus diesem Grunde sind auch andere Umstellungen, die du vom Deutschen her kennst, im Englischen nicht möglich:

Heute	habe	ich	Kopfweh.	Today	I	have	got a headache.
Heute	bin	ich	krank.	Today	I	am	ill.
	Verb	**Subjekt**			**Subjekt**	**Verb**	

Merke: Im englischen Aussagesatz steht das Subjekt immer vor dem Verb. Es wird auch dann nicht umgestellt, wenn ihm ein anderer Satzteil vorausgeht.

ÜBUNG 1 What you can do or say

Write as many sentences as you can. Begin with the subordinate clause.
Example: Before I go to school, I usually do my homework.

What do you	say do think	before you go to school? when you don't want to go to school? when it's too cold to get up? when you are late? when you must do your homework? when you must go to bed? before you get up? before you have breakfast? when you go to bed? when you can't find your homework?

ÜBUNG 2 A week in Jenny's life

Jenny always takes down in a calendar what she wants to do. This is a week in her life. Ask Jenny what she is going to do.

Example: What are you going to do on Monday, Jenny? Well, let me see …
On Monday, I …

Monday:	4 p.m. table tennis with Tom
Tuesday:	8.15 p.m. watch film on TV
Wednesday:	after school learn for German test with Tom
Thursday:	6 p.m. help Kate with maths homework
Friday:	5 p.m. buy birthday present for Sarah/ring up Sarah
Saturday:	Sarah's birthday party at 2 p.m.
Sunday:	ring up Tom/go for a walk with Tom at 4 p.m.

ÜBUNG 3 Your plans

What are your plans for the next week? What are you going to do on Monday, Tuesday, etc?

Example: On Monday, I'm going to play football.
On Tuesday, …

Go on.

ÜBUNG 4

Tom's homework

For his German homework, Tom must write eight sentences in German. Here they are. Can you put them into English?

Homework

1. Heute bin ich krank.
2. Heute muss ich nicht aufstehen.
3. Heute kann ich im Bett bleiben.
4. Heute muss ich nicht in die Schule gehen.
5. Heute muss ich keine Hausaufgaben machen.
6. Heute habe ich kein Deutsch.
7. Heute habe ich Fieber.
8. Heute ist ein schöner Tag.

REGEL

Die Stellung der Objekte

Tom	has got	a sister.
He	likes	her.
He	is buying	her an ice cream.
She	likes	ice cream.
He	must buy	an ice cream for Timmy, too.
Subjekt	**Verb**	**Objekt**

Objekte stehen im Englischen immer nach dem Verb oder der Verbgruppe. Im Englischen dürfen keine Satzteile zwischen dem Verb und dem Objekt stehen.

ÜBUNG 5

At the school cafeteria

Not all the pupils like what they can eat at the school cafeteria. Mike, for example, doesn't like beans. What about the others? Complete what they say

Sarah:

Brr ...! Pudding again.

I really ____________ . Why isn't there any ice cream?

Christine:

Ugh ...! Sausages.

I ____________ yesterday.

I can't ____________ every day.

Joe:

Look at those eggs. I ____________ this morning. I ____________ another egg now.

Tom:

I ____________ chocolate pudding.

If you don't want your chocolate pudding, you ____________ to me.

Sandra to Kevin:

For me it's chips. I could ____________ from morning to night.

Kevin:

What about this fruit salad? I think I'll ____________ . ____________ you ____________ fruit salad, too, Sandra?

REGEL

Die Stellung von Zeit- und Ortsangaben

	Tom	gets up		at 6.30.
	He	leaves	home	after breakfast.
Today	he	walks	to school.	
In England	school	starts		at 8.30.
Zeit/Ort			**Ort**	**Zeit**

Zeitangaben stehen meist am Ende des Satzes. Wenn sie am Satzanfang stehen, sind sie stärker betont. Auch Ortsangaben können am Satzanfang stehen.
Wenn Zeit- und Ortsangaben zusammentreffen, steht die Ortsangabe immer vor der Zeitangabe.

ÜBUNG 6 Schools in England

Schools in England are different. Here is some information about schools in England. Put the words in the right order.

1. already go/English pupils/when they are five/to school
2. go to a comprehensive school/most British pupils/when they are eleven
3. when they are 16/school/they can leave
4. school uniform/in many schools/they must wear
5. are blue and grey/the school colours/in Tom's school
6. the school uniforms/in special shops/can buy/the pupils' parents
7. later than in Germany/in most English schools/begin lessons
8. lessons/in the afternoon/most English pupils have/also
9. school cafeterias/many English schools/so/there are lessons also in the afternoon/have
10. lunch/pupils/can have/during break/at the school cafeteria
11. In many English schools/learn/pupils/to cook

ÜBUNG 7 Tom's timetable

This is Tom's timetable for Monday.

9.15	– 9.55	Maths
9.55	– 10.35	Maths
10.35	– 10.50	Break
10.50	– 11.30	Biology
11.30	– 12.10	Biology
12.10	– 1.45	Lunch break
1.45	– 2.25	Geography
2.25	– 3.05	English
3.05	– 3.45	German

Now ask Tom

– what subjects he has on Monday.
– what he has in the first, second … lesson.
– what he does in the break.
– what he does from 1.45 to 2.25.
– when and where he sees Jenny.
– if he has lunch in the school cafeteria.
– when he does his homework.
– where he does his homework.

Example: What subjects do you have on Monday?
– Well, on Monday I have …

REGEL

Die Stellung der Adverbien der Häufigkeit

Unter Adverbien der Häufigkeit versteht man Ausdrücke wie *often, always, sometimes, never, usually* u.a. Sie geben an, wie oft man bestimmte Dinge tut. Im Englischen stehen die Adverbien der Häufigkeit:

a) im *simple present* vor dem Verb,	Tom usually does his homework at home. He sometimes forgets his homework.
b) bei Hilfsverben, denen ein Infinitiv oder ein *past participle* folgt, vor dem Infinitiv/ *past participle*,	He must always help his sister. She has never done his home work.
c) im *simple present* und *simple past* nach den Formen von *to be*, sonst wie unter b).	Timmy isn't often ill. He was sometimes ill last year. But he has never been really ill.

Beachte: *Sometimes* kann auch am Satzanfang stehen, wenn es besonders betont ist:

Sometimes Tom forgets his homework.

ÜBUNG 8 **Homework**

Put in often, usually, etc.

	who	forget	their homework.
	who	have	forgotten their homework.
	who	do	their homework at school.
	who	have	copied it from their neighbours.
There are pupils	who	know	what they must do.
	who	write	down what they must do.
	who	forget	their homework at home.
	who	do	it on the way to school.
	who	leave	their exercise book at home.
	who	forget	it on the bus.

usually sometimes never always never
never often sometimes never usually

ÜBUNG 9

You and your homework

Answer in full sentences. Use always, often, etc. in your answers.

1. What about your homework? Do you usually do it?
2. When do you usually do it?
3. Where do you do it?
4. Do you often forget it?
5. Why do you sometimes forget it?
6. Do you often copy it from your neighbour?
7. Are you usually busy in the breaks?
8. Does your neighbour/your mum/your dad often help you with your homework?
9. In what subjects does he or she often help you?
10. Has your teacher ever helped you?

RECHTSCHREIBUNG

Liebe Schülerin, lieber Schüler,

im vorangegangenen Teil „Grammatik“ hast du zusätzlich zu den Grammatikregeln auch viele Rechtschreibregeln gelernt, die dir helfen, im Diktat besser zu werden – z. B. Besonderheiten in der Schreibung vor der Endung *-s* im *simple present* und vor der Endung *-ed* im *simple past*.

Im Teil „Rechtschreibung“ haben wir nun weitere wichtige Stolpersteine der englischen Rechtschreibung zusammengestellt. Du findest in den Kapiteln abwechslungsreiche Übungen, einprägsame Regeln und Warnungen vor gefährlichen Fehlerquellen. Zu jedem Kapitel gehören auch ein oder mehrere Diktate. Die Diktattexte sind in dem Teil „Diktate“ abgedruckt.

Am besten gehst du bei jedem Kapitel folgendermaßen vor:

- Als Erstes prägst du dir die Regeln ein und bearbeitest die dazugehörigen Übungen. Die Lösungen zu den Übungen findest du im Lösungsteil.
- Anschließend schreibst du das Diktat. Lass dir den Text vorlesen. Das Ergebnis in dem Diktat zeigt dir, ob du alle Regeln in dem Kapitel verstanden und behalten hast.
- Als Letztes kommen die Verbesserungen: Du schreibst jedes Wort, das du im Diktat falsch geschrieben hast, noch einmal richtig auf – am besten mit dem (Teil-)Satz, in dem es im Diktat vorkam. Das betreffende Wort solltest du dabei farbig hervorheben.

Wenn du dir die Listen mit den Verbesserungen vor jeder Klassenarbeit nochmals gründlich durchliest, wirst du bestimmt viele Fehler vermeiden können!

Wörter mit „o“/„oo“

1

ÜBUNG 1 Setze die richtigen Wörter ein.

It’s a … 

It’s a … 

It’s not new, it’s … .

One and one is … .

They’re … and sister.

It’s a … 

		o				
	o	o				
o						
		o				
		o				
	o	o				

ÜBUNG 2 In jedem der drei Sätze steckt ein Druckfehler.
Streiche das falsche Wort durch und schreibe das richtige darüber.

a) God morning, John.

b) Tom: “Is the cat in the hause?”

c) Tom’s mather is at home.

ÜBUNG 3 Sieh dir die Bilder an, lies die Fragen und beantworte sie. Verwende dabei Kurzformen.

Beispiel: What’s this? It’s a book.

Übung 3 / Diktat

1. Where are the books?

____

____

2. What's this?

____

3. How old is Daisy?

____

4. Where's the teddy?

____

5. Is Peter in the garden?

No, ______________________________

____

6. Is the girl at home?

No, ______________________________

____

DIKTAT 14

Und jetzt solltest du als Abschluss dieses Kapitels ein kurzes Diktat schreiben. Lass dir den Text diktieren – Diktat Nr. 14.
Achtung: Das Wort „mother" muss in diesem Text großgeschrieben werden. Es wird wie ein Eigenname verwendet.

2 Die Zahlen bis 100 – Die Uhrzeit

Ehe du die folgenden Übungen machst, solltest du die Ordnungszahlen in deinem Lehrbuch wiederholen.

Die Zahlen von 1 bis 20

ÜBUNG 1 Wenn du die Kästchen ausfüllst, erhältst du Zahlen von eins bis fünfzehn.

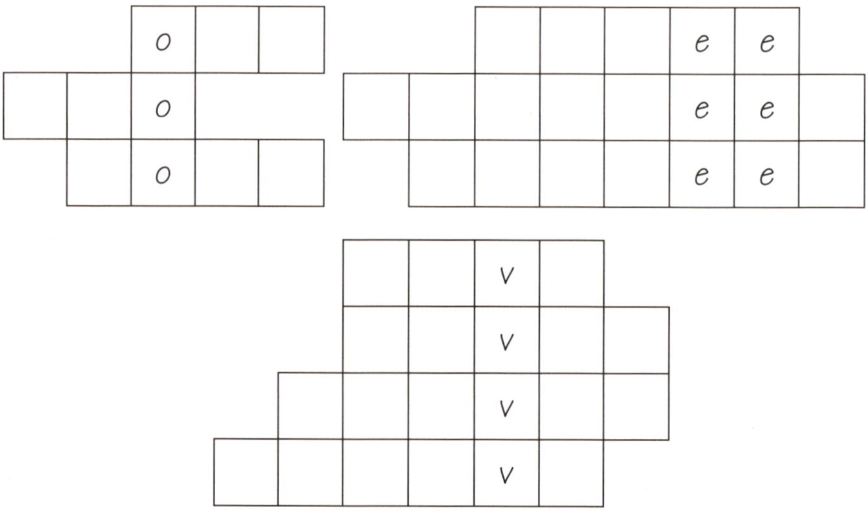

ÜBUNG 2 Welche Zahlen von eins bis zehn reimen sich auf die folgenden Wörter?

late – __________ floor – __________

too – __________ (to) drive – __________

pen – __________ (to) shine – __________

key – __________ (He) picks – __________

ÜBUNG 3

Buchstabenspiele mit Zahlwörtern

a) Welches Zahlwort steckt in „telephone?“ __________

b) Nimm von dem gesuchten Zahlwort einen Buchstaben weg und du erhältst einen „Baum“. __________

c) In diesem Zahlwort steckt der englische Vorname „Eve“. __________

d) Ersetze den ersten Buchstaben dieses Zahlwortes und du erhältst ein Fragepronomen. __________

e) Ersetze den ersten Buchstaben dieses Zahlwortes durch einen anderen und du erhältst 60 Minuten. (Achtung: Die Aussprache ändert sich!) __________

f) Wenn du den ersten Buchstaben dieses Zahlwortes durch einen anderen ersetzt, erhältst du ein Possessivpronomen. (Achtung: Die Aussprache ändert sich!) __________

g) In welchem Zahlwort steckt eine Präposition? (Hilfestellung: Sie drückt das Gegenteil von „under“ aus.) __________

h) Streiche den ersten und den letzten Buchstaben dieses Zahlwortes, und du erhältst wieder eine Präposition. __________

i) Streiche den mittleren Buchstaben dieses Zahlwortes, und du erhältst eine Präposition, die man leicht mit „too“ verwechselt. __________

ÜBUNG 4

Ergänze und achte auf die Veränderungen in der Schreibung:

a) five + teen → ____________

b) eight + teen → ____________

Die Zahlen von 20 bis 100

ÜBUNG 5

Ergänze die Zehnerzahlen nach folgendem Muster:

two – twenty____________ six – ____________

three – ____________ seven – ____________

four (!) – ____________ eight – ____________

five (!) – ____________ nine – ____________

ten (!) – a ____________

ÜBUNG 6

a) Ergänze nach folgendem Muster:

six – sixteen____________ – sixty____________

five – ____________ – ____________

four – ____________ – ____________

b) Ergänze die Reihe bis 55.

twenty-two, thirty-three, ______-______, ______-______.

c) Vorsicht! Ein „falscher“ Freund! einhundert = one hundre____

ÜBUNG 7

Du bist mit deinen Eltern in England. Deine Eltern wollen mit Schecks bezahlen, sie können aber nicht so gut englische Zahlen schreiben wie du. Hilf ihnen beim Ausfüllen der Schecks.

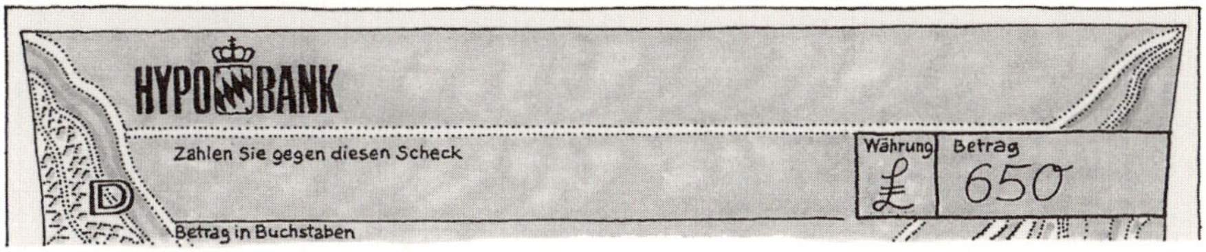

oder:

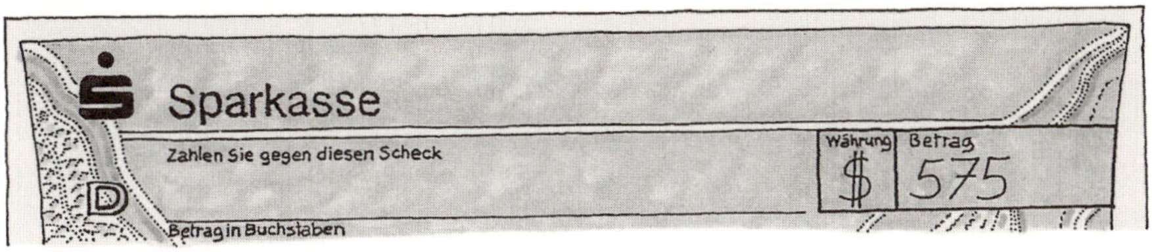

Die Uhrzeit

ACHTUNG

Du hast im Unterricht in der Schule sicher schon die englischen Uhrzeiten gelernt. Hier nun noch einmal zur Erinnerung:

It's five o'clock.	– Es ist fünf Uhr.
It's half past seven.	– Es ist halb acht.
It's (a) quarter past nine.	– Es ist Viertel nach neun.
It's (a) quarter to twelve.	– Es ist Viertel vor zwölf.
It's five (minutes) past three.	– Es ist fünf (Minuten) nach drei.
It's five (minutes) to nine.	– Es ist fünf (Minuten) vor neun.

ÜBUNG

8 Ergänze die Sätze.

a) What time is it? – It's seven ___________.

b) A minute has 60 ___________.

c) It's five minutes ___________nine. *(8.55)*

d) It's ___________ past nine. *(9.30)*

e) It's a ___________ to ten. *(9.45)*

ÜBUNG

9 Hier ist eine Uhrzeit in Lautschrift. Wie viel Uhr mag es wohl sein?

It's [tu:tətu:]

It's ________________.

ÜBUNG

10 Stumme Buchstaben *(silent letters)* kennst du schon. Ergänze die Wörter.

a) It's a qua____ter to eleven.

b) You must wait ha____f an ____our.

DIKTAT

15 Und jetzt solltest du als Abschluss dieses Kapitels ein kurzes Diktat schreiben. Lass dir den Text diktieren – Diktat Nr. 15.

3

Wörter mit „o“/„oo“/„ou“

Der Buchstabe **o** kann auf verschiedene Weise ausgesprochen werden. Sprich dir die folgenden Wörter laut vor.

Aussprache:

langes **u:** [u:] two
Doppellaut: [əʊ] no
kurzes **a:** [ʌ] come

Du kennst auch Wörter, die mit **oo** geschrieben, aber wie ein kurzes **u** [u] ausgesprochen werden; z. B. good.

Es gibt aber auch Wörter mit **oo**, die wie ein langes, offenes **o** [ɔ:] ausgesprochen werden, z. B. floor.

Das Ganze ist nicht so kompliziert wie es klingt und wenn du die folgenden Übungen sorgfältig machst, wirst du die Schreibung von Wörtern mit **o**, **oo** oder **ou** bald beherrschen.

ÜBUNG **1**

Welche der folgenden Wörter spricht man mit einem langen **u** [u:] und welche mit einem kurzen **u** [u] aus?

Versuche dich zu erinnern: Wie hat der Lehrer oder die Lehrerin diese Wörter im Unterricht ausgesprochen? (Eine kleine Hilfe für dich: mit kurzem **u** [u] spricht man drei Wörter aus der Liste aus.)

Schreibe die passenden Wörter neben die Lautzeichen.

boot, school, good, two, who, book, afternoon, shoe, too, look

[u:]: ______________________________

[u]: ______________________________

ÜBUNG 2

Sprich dir die Wörter laut vor und schreibe das Wort, das nicht in die Reihe gehört, an den Rand.

a) house – about – our – your ______________________

b) hello – biro – now – window ______________________

c) shop – box – woman – not ______________________

d) come – some – home – mother ______________________

e) four – house – our – about ______________________

ÜBUNG 3

Die folgende Wortliste enthält jeweils zwei Wörter, die den gleichen Laut enthalten, der jedoch verschieden geschrieben wird.

Schreibe die beiden Wörter neben die Lautsymbole, sprich sie dir laut vor und präge dir ein, wie der gleiche Laut auf verschiedene Weise geschrieben wird.

Beispiel: Sage dir laut vor: „floor" schreibt man mit zwei **o**, „four" schreibt man mit **ou**.

floor – biro – foot – four – woman – too – window – two

offenes „o" [ɔ:]: floor ______________ four ______________

Doppellaut [əʊ]: ______________ ______________

kurzes „u" [u]: ______________ ______________

langes „u" [u:]: ______________ ______________

ÜBUNG 4

Wenn du das Kreuzworträtsel richtig ausfüllst, so ergeben die dunklen Kästchen eine Großstadt, in der der Buchstabe **o** zweimal vorkommt, aber jedes Mal anders ausgesprochen wird.
(Setze nur englische Wörter ein.)

1. Das sagst du, wenn du jemand etwas zeigen willst.
2. Höfliche Menschen machen sie immer zu.
3. Zum Raus-, Rein- und Durchsehen.
4. Dieses Wort findet man oft vor dem Morgen und vor dem Abend.
5. Wenn sie mit Wasser gefüllt ist, ist sie harmlos.
6. Die beste Zeit zum Spielen und zum Hausaufgabenmachen.

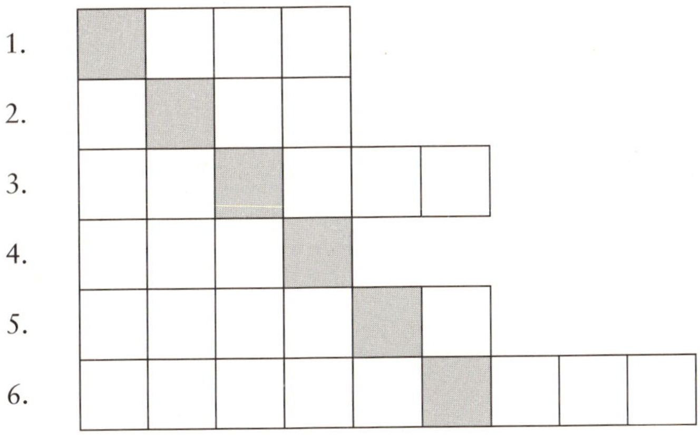

REGEL

Die Wörter **two** und **too** werden gleich ausgesprochen [tu:], aber verschieden geschrieben.

Auch die Bedeutungen (two = zwei, too = auch) sind verschieden.

Um Fehler zu vermeiden, musst du überlegen, welche Bedeutung in den jeweiligen Satz passt.

ÜBUNG 5

Setze „two“ oder „too“ ein.

“Have you got one or _______ brothers?“ –

“I’ve got _______ brothers.”

“Have you got a sister, _______?” –

“No, I haven’t.”

Da bei diesen Wörtern häufig Fehler gemacht werden, wollen wir noch eine zweite Übung machen.

ÜBUNG 6

Bitte denke nochmals mit: Welches Wort passt von seiner Bedeutung her in die Sätze?

“There’s a circus in town with tigers and elephants and crocodiles.” –

“Oh, crocodiles, _______? How many?” –

“_______ or three, I think.”

“Great. Let’s go there.”

Zum Abschluss dieser Übungen noch eine kleine Hilfestellung für dich: „too“ mit der Bedeutung „auch“ steht meistens am Ende eines Satzes.

DIKTAT 16

Und jetzt solltest du als Abschluss dieses Kapitels ein kurzes Diktat schreiben. Lass dir den Text diktieren – Diktat Nr. 16.

4 Farben – Kleidungsstücke

Farben

ÜBUNG 1 Die ausgefüllten Kästchen ergeben Farben.

On a sunny day the sky is					*e*				
On a rainy day the sky is					*e*				
On a snowy day everything is					*e*				
In summer the grass is					*e*				
In winter our noses are often					*e*				
What colour is a sunflower?					*e*				

ÜBUNG 2 Ergänze die Antworten.

a) What colour is chocolate? – It's ________________.

b) What colour is between white and red? – It's ________________.

c) What colour is coffee without milk or cream? – It's ________________.

ÜBUNG **3** Ergänze.

a) What colour is …

– a canary? – It's __________.

– a penguin? – It's __________

and __________.

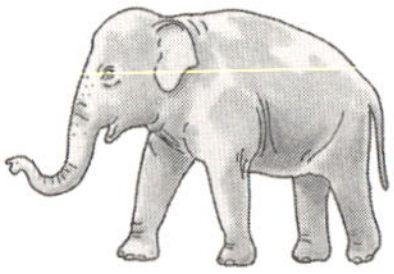

– an elephant? – It's __________.

– a polar bear? – It's __________.

Eine nicht ganz ernst gemeinte Frage!

b) What colour ist a man before and after he swims in cold water?

He's ________ before and ________ after.

Kleidungsstücke

ÜBUNG **4** Schreibe die Namen dieser Kleidungsstücke auf.

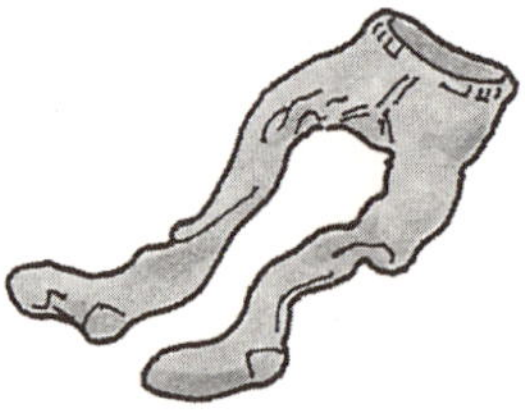

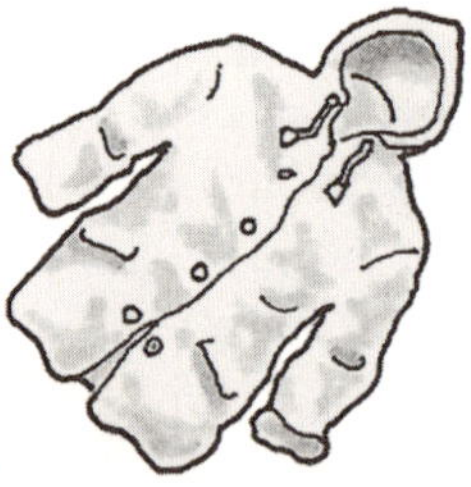

________________ ________________ ________________

ÜBUNG 5

Die folgenden Kleidungsstücke stehen alle im Plural. Welche davon bestehen aus zwei Teilen, so dass man „a pair of" davor stellen kann?

jackets, sandals, raincoats, dresses, jeans, socks, skirts, wellies, stockings, tights, sunhats, blouses, shorts, T-shirts

a pair of ______________ a pair of ______________

a pair of ______________ a pair of ______________

a pair of ______________ a pair of ______________

„too" heißt erstens „auch" (Is your brother coming, too?) und zweitens „zu". (This coat is too expensive.)

ÜBUNG 6

Ergänze.

too long, too short, too big, too small

The boy's ______________

and __________ are too short.

His __________ are too big.

The girl's ______________

and __________ are too long.

Her ______________ is too small.

Zum Abschluss noch eine (leichte) Frage: Es gibt zwei Kleidungsstücke, die sich in der Schreibung nur durch einen Buchstaben unterscheiden.
Eines davon tragen Männer oder Jungen und Frauen oder Mädchen. Das andere Kleidungsstück tragen nur Frauen oder Mädchen (außer in Schottland!).
Schreibe sie zu den Namen:

Kevin's __________

Kate's __________

DIKTAT

17

Und jetzt solltest du als Abschluss dieses Kapitels ein kurzes Diktat schreiben. Lass dir den Text diktieren – Diktat Nr. 17.

5 Besondere Schreibweisen

Hier üben wir Wörter, bei denen besonders häufig Fehler gemacht werden:

1. Zusammensetzungen mit „all“ und „full“
2. „of“ oder „off“
3. Wörter, bei denen Schreibung und Aussprache erheblich abweichen.

REGEL

Zusammensetzungen mit „all“ und „full“

all + so	→	also (auch)	ein l entfällt!
all + most	→	almost (fast)	
all + ready	→	already (schon)	
all + ways	→	always (immer)	
care + full	→	careful (vorsichtig)	ein l entfällt!
use + full	→	useful (nützlich)	
wonder + full	→	wonderful (wunderbar)	

ÜBUNG

1 Ergänze die Sätze.

a) The weather is ________________ today. *(wonder + full)*

b) Kevin ________________ goes to school by bus. *(all + ways)*

c) A washing-machine is very ________________. *(use + full)*

d) In this shop you can buy ________________ everything. *(all + most)*

e) Mr Bennett is a _______________ driver. *(care + full)*

f) It's seven o'clock and Molly is _______________ in bed. *(all + ready)*

g) Does your friend _______________ play table tennis? *(all + so)*

ACHTUNG

of oder **off** werden häufig verwechselt; **of** gibt an, zu welcher Sache etwas gehört (of-Genitiv)

Beispiel: The door of the house is closed.

off steht nach bestimmten Verben:

(to) get off (aussteigen)
(to) take off (ausziehen von Kleidungsstücken)
(to) run off (weglaufen)

ÜBUNG 2 Ergänze die folgenden Sätze:

a) Where's the end _______ the street?

b) It's warm today, you can take your pullover _______.

c) You must get _______ at the next bus stop.

d) Mr Johnson's shop is on the corner _______ the street.

e) What's the name _______ this town?

f) When Molly's cat sees the neighbour's dog, she always runs _______.

ÜBUNG 3

Ordne die vertauschten Buchstaben der Wörter.

Achtung: In jedem der Wörter mit vertauschten Buchstaben ist ein Buchstabe, der nicht dazu passt.
Schreibe diese überflüssigen Buchstaben in die Zeile am Ende der Übung und du erhältst ein Wort, das ganz anders gesprochen als geschrieben wird.

a) What ourloca ________________ is the children's rabbit? – It's white.

b) Tom and Betty ugulah ________________ at Molly's dirty cat.

c) The boy is too fat, he can't climb gorthuth ________________ the small window.

d) Our inugehurob ________________ is a very friendly man.

e) The Parkers have eggs and samguesas ________________ for breakfast.

f) Scotland is a nelutaifub ________________ country.

Eine kleine Hilfestellung für dich: das Wort, das du suchst, bezeichnet eine Jahreszeit.
Die überflüssigen Buchstaben sind: ____ ____ ____ ____ ____ ____

DIKTAT 18

Und jetzt solltest du als Abschluss dieses Kapitels ein kurzes Diktat schreiben. Lass dir den Text diktieren – Diktat Nr. 18.

6 Groß- und Kleinschreibung

Im Englischen werden die meisten Wörter klein geschrieben, die man im Deutschen groß schreibt.

Beispiel: In the shop, people buy fruit. (Im Laden kaufen die Leute Obst.)

Bestimmte Wörter werden jedoch im Englischen immer großgeschrieben.

Im folgenden Kasten findest du die Regeln für die Groß- und Kleinschreibung im Englischen. Achte besonders auf die mit einem x versehenen Beispiele, bei denen die deutsche Rechtschreibung von der englischen abweicht!

REGEL

Es werden großgeschrieben:	Im Englischen wie im Deutschen?	
1. Personennamen:	Jason Smith	✔
2. Verwandtschaftsbezeichnungen als Bestandteile von Eigennamen:	Uncle Jack; Aunt(ie) Chris	✔
aber **nicht** *brother, sister, cousin*	This is my brother Tom / sister Sue	✘
Verwandtschaftsnamen als Ersatz für einen Eigennamen in der Anrede:	Hi, Mum; Hello, Grandad!	✔
nicht aber, wenn sie nur als Substantiv verwendet werden:	Her aunt / my dad works here.	✘
3. Orts- und Ländernamen:	in London / Germany; the River Avon	✔

4. Himmelsrichtungen in Orts- / und Ländernamen:	I live in North London / South Africa	✔
sonst aber **nicht**:	We drove to the west.	✘
5. Sprachen als Substantive:	He speaks English and French.	✔
6. Eigenschaftswörter für Länder / Sprachen:	a German car; an English dictation	✘
7. Wochentage und Monatsnamen:	on Monday; last August	✔
nicht aber die Jahreszeiten:	spring, summer, autumn, winter	✘
8. Feste und Feiertage:	Christmas; Easter *(Ostern)*; Halloween	✔

ÜBUNG 1

Ein kleines Quiz. Kannst du alle Sätze richtig ergänzen?

a) Edinburgh is the capital of Scotland.

b) The shortest month in the year is ______________.

c) You get presents from your relatives and friends on your ______________.

d) We give each other presents at ______________.

e) Your mother's father is your ______________.

f) The coldest time of the year is ______________.

g) My mother's brother is my ______________.

h) The Rolls Royce is an ______________ car.

i) In France the people speak ______________.

j) Every ______________ many people go to church.

ÜBUNG 2

In Zeitungsüberschriften wird alles groß geschrieben. Schreibe folgende „Headlines“ (Überschriften) in normaler Schrift nochmals ab, so als stünden sie *in* dem Zeitungsartikel.

a) **BIG FIRE AT SUPERMARKET IN OXFORD STREET**

b) **NO TRAINS TO SOUTH WALES TODAY**

c) **COLDEST CHRISTMAS SINCE WINTER OF 1989**

d) **MORE GERMAN SPORTS CARS ON BRITAIN'S ROADS**

e) **FEWER JOBS IN THE SOUTH OF ENGLAND**

f) **BABY TINA'S DAD IS 84!**

g) **MANY MORE FISH IN THE RIVER THAMES**

a) Big fire at supermarket in Oxford Street

b) ______________________________

c) ______________________________

d) ______________________________

e) ______________________________

f) ______________________________

g) ______________________________

ACHTUNG

In Briefen beginnt der erste Satz nach der Anrede immer mit einem Großbuchstaben, obwohl nach der Anrede im britischen Englisch ein Komma, im amerikanischen Englisch ein Doppelpunkt steht:

	British English	American English
	Dear Uncle Jim,	Hi, Snoopy:
	We are here in G …	The weather here is …
Auch der Anfang vom Abschluss wird immer großgeschrieben:	Thats all my news,	Please write soon,
	Yours, Vicky	All the best, Debbie

ÜBUNG 3

Ergänze den Brief auf der nächsten Seite mit den Wörtern in der „Wolke“. Achte dabei auf die richtige Schreibweise: groß oder klein!

LETTER I EASTER DEAR STREET
GERMANY THIS ENGLAND SPRING
MAY LOVE WEDNESDAY UNCLE YOU

23, High Street,

Brighton

____________ BN1 4PE

____________ 3rd ____________

____________ ____________ Alex,

____________ is not going to be a long ____________! ____________ hope that ____________ and your family are all OK. The weather here is fine but it is still a bit cold for ____________. We were in France for a week during the ____________ holidays. Did you have a nice time in Berlin? I have never been to ____________ but it must be a nice country. Well, that's all my news for today,

____________,

Barbara

ACHTUNG

Das Datum im Englischen

Das Datum wird im Englischen anders geschrieben als gesprochen. Dabei gibt es folgende Möglichkeiten:

Schreibung	Aussprache
July 1st	July the first
July 1	July the first
1st July	the first of July
1 July	the first of July

ÜBUNG **4** Wie schreiben die Kinder das Datum auf die Einladung zu ihrer Geburtstagsparty? (Wähle eine der 4 Schreibweisen aus.)

a) Kevins Party ist am Freitag, dem 8. April.

My birthday party is on ______________________.

I hope you can come.

b) Kates Party ist am Sonntag, dem 17. Juli.

My birthday party is on ______________________.

You must come.

c) Toms Party ist am Samstag, dem 12. Oktober.

Can you come to my birthday party? It's on ______________________.

d) Betty ist am 29. Februar geboren. Dieses Jahr ist kein Schaltjahr, daher feiert sie ihren Geburtstag einen Tag vorher, nämlich an einem Mittwoch.

____.

Please come.

DIKTATE 19 20 21

Zu diesem Kapitel gibt es 3 Diktate: Nr. 19, 20 und 21.

In dem Diktat Nr. 21 kommt ein Wort vor, dessen Schreibweise du vielleicht noch nicht kennst – bis auf die Kleinschreibung entspricht sie der deutschen:

café = Café

7 Falsche Freunde

„Falsche Freunde“ sind Freunde, auf die man sich nicht verlassen kann. Das gilt im wirklichen Leben wie beim Erlernen einer Fremdsprache. Du kannst dich z. B. nicht darauf verlassen, dass man auch im Englischen ein tragbares Telefon als „Handy“ oder ein altes Auto als „Oldtimer“ bezeichnet, einfach weil diese englischen Wörter im Deutschen benutzt werden. Statt „Handy“ sagt man im Englischen „mobile“ oder „cellphone“, und ein „oldtimer“ ist ein Mensch, meistens ein alter Cowboy.
In diesem Kapitel werden wir uns aber vorwiegend mit englischen Wörtern beschäftigen, bei denen die Ähnlichkeit in der Schreibung zu den gleichbedeutenden deutschen Wörtern zu Flüchtigkeitsfehlern im Diktat führen könnte.

ACHTUNG

Viele englische Substantive werden – bis auf die Kleinschreibung – wie im Deutschen geschrieben, z. B. **butter, café, margarine, match, pool, show, winter, wind.** Hier lauert die Gefahr, dass man im englischen Diktat den Anfangsbuchstaben aus Versehen großschreibt!

Der Unterschied zwischen Groß- und und Kleinschreibung ist bei den Monatsnamen kein Problem: Sie werden im Englischen wie im Deutschen großgeschrieben. Die englischen Monatsnamen sind überhaupt den deutschen sehr ähnlich. Die folgende Übung beschäftigt sich mit ihrer Schreibweise.

ÜBUNG 1

Ergänze die Monatsnamen im unten stehenden Kalender. Bei den freien Feldern ist die Schreibweise anders als im Deutschen, aber auch bei den vorgegebenen Monaten sind in zwei Fällen Änderungen nötig. Die erste haben wir bereits als Beispiel für dich vorgenommen.

Januar**y**	Februar		April		
	August	September		November	

Das Wort „Kalender" heißt übrigens „calendar" im Englischen und ist somit in zweifacher Hinsicht ein „falscher Freund". Und wo wir gerade beim Kalender sind: Verwechsle nicht „Easter" (Ostern) mit „Eastern" (Ost-, östlich)!

Wörter wie „calendar" sind sehr fehlerträchtig, weil sie Laute enthalten, die zwar im Deutschen und Englischen gleich ausgesprochen (in diesem Fall [k]), aber unterschiedlich geschrieben werden: Das deutsche „K" in „Kalender" entspricht hier dem englischen „c" in „calendar".

Im folgenden Achtung-Kasten findest du weitere Beispiele.

ACHTUNG

Gleiche Aussprache, andere Schreibweise

1. Das deutsche **k** wird im Englischen meist zu **c**.

Beispiele:	**Deutsch**	**Englisch**
	Doktor	doctor
	Amerika	America
	perfekt	perfect

2. Das deutsche **sch** wird im Englischen fast immer zu **sh**.

Beispiele:	**Deutsch**	**Englisch**
	englisch	English
	Schock	shock
	waschen	wash

Ausnahme: Die einzigen Wörter, die du bisher (und bis auf Weiteres) kennst, die im Englischen mit **sch** geschrieben werden, sind Verbindungen mit „**sch**ool", wobei das **sch** als [sk] gesprochen wird.

3. Bei einigen Nomen entspricht die deutsche Endung **-er** im britischen Englisch der Endung **-re**.

Beispiele:	**Deutsch**	**brit. Englisch**
	Center	centre
	Theater	theatre
	Liter	litre
	Meter	metre

ÜBUNG **2**

Schreibe die englische Übersetzung neben das deutsche Wort.

a) Doktor	doctor	g) exakt	______
b) korrekt	______	h) britisch	______
c) perfekt	______	i) Physik	______s
d) Theater	______	j) schottisch	______
e) Musik	______	k) Fisch	______
f) Subjekt	______	l) Picknick	______

Eine weitere Fehlerquelle in Diktaten sind Wörter, die im Englischen „einen Tick anders" geschrieben werden als im Deutschen.

ACHTUNG

1. Der deutschen Endung **-ie** entspricht im Englischen oft die Endung **-y**.

Beispiele:

Deutsch	Englisch
Chemie	chemistry
Familie	family
Geographie	geography

2. Ein **Doppelbuchstabe** im Deutschen entspricht in vielen Fällen einem **Einzelbuchstaben** im Englischen.

Beispiele:

Deutsch	Englisch
Mann	man
beginnen	begin
schwimmen	swim

Denk daran, dass im Englischen Verben wie „swim" und „begin" ihren Endkonsonanten nur vor bestimmten Endungen verdoppeln (siehe Kapitel 3).

3. Es gibt aber auch Fälle, in denen ein **Einzelbuchstabe** im Deutschen einem **Doppelbuchstaben** im Englischen entspricht.

Beispiele:

Deutsch	Englisch
Adresse	address
Glas	glass
Gras	grass

Nicht alle Wörter, die im Englischen „einen Tick anders" geschrieben werden als im Deutschen, lassen sich in Gruppen zusammenfassen. Manche dieser Wörter, von denen auch einige in der folgenden Übung vorkommen, musst du einfach einzeln lernen.

ÜBUNG 3

Du kennst sicher die englischen Übersetzungen für folgende deutsche Wörter. Aber kannst du sie auch richtig schreiben?

a) Banane	banana	j) Medizin	________
b) Marmelade	________	k) bevor	________
c) schwamm	________	l) Sommer	________
d) Glas	________	m) Familie	________
e) Tee	________	n) Postkarte	________
f) Assistent	________	o) Gruppe	________
g) Kaffee	________	p) Suppe	________
h) Magazin	________	q) Schokolade	________
i) hundert	________	r) Tomate	________

ACHTUNG

Merke dir besonders diejenigen englischen Wörter, die im Gegensatz zum Deutschen ein „stummes End-**e**" haben, z. B. before, detective, magazine, medicine, temperature.

DIKTAT 22

Zum Abschluss dieses Kapitels solltest du ein Diktat schreiben. Lass dir den Text diktieren – Diktat Nr. 22.

In dem Diktat kommen zwei Begriffe vor, die du vielleicht noch nicht kennst:

orchestra = Orchester
fruit juice [fru:t dʒu:s] = Fruchtsaft

Merke dir die Schreibweise dieser Wörter gut.

8 Gleich und ähnlich klingende Wörter

Nichts an einem Diktat ist heimtückischer als das Vorhandensein von Wörtern, die zwar gleich (oder ähnlich) ausgesprochen werden, jedoch eine völlig andere Bedeutung haben und auch ganz anders geschrieben werden! Hierzu gibt es keine Rechtschreibregeln. Hier hilft nur eines: sich die unterschiedliche Schreibweise der oft ähnlich geschriebenen Wörter merken und immer an den Zusammenhang im Satz und an die eigentliche Bedeutung der Wörter denken!

Gleich klingende Wörter

ÜBUNG 1

Vervollständige die Liste unten mit dem jeweils gleich klingenden Wort. Sprich dir dazu jedes Wort laut vor.

a) red	read	i) I	____
b) blew	____	j) knows	____
c) through	____	k) two	____
d) new	____	l) weak	____
e) road	____	m) eight	____
f) wood	____	n) wear	____
g) break	____	o) meat	____
h) here	____	p) their	____

Falls du ein Wort aus der Übung nicht kennen solltest, schlage es in deinem Englischbuch (oder einem Wörterbuch) nach. Es handelt sich um sehr wichtige Wörter, die gern von Englischlehrern in Diktate eingebaut werden!

Tipp

Stelle eine Liste aller gleich klingenden Wörter in Übung 1 zusammen und trage sie in dein Vokabelheft ein. Lass eine Doppelseite im Vokabelheft frei und ergänze deine Liste immer, wenn du ein neues Wort lernst, das die gleiche Aussprache wie ein dir bekanntes hat.

Auf diese Weise schaffst du dir selbst eine wichtige Hilfe für die Diktatnoten-Schlacht!

ACHTUNG

Besondere Vorsicht ist bei Wörtern geboten, die sogar *drei* unterschiedliche Schreibweisen haben! Hier musst du besonders auf den Zusammenhang achten.
Im Folgenden einige wichtige Hinweise zu typischen Verwendungen:

to / too / two

> "I want to have two sausages, too!"

to: Das Wort „to" wird entweder als Präposition ("I'm talking to John") oder vor dem Infinitiv benutzt.

two: Das Zahlwort „two" steht natürlich meist vor einer Mehrzahlform.

too: Das Wort „too" steht in der Bedeutung „auch" meist nach Komma am Satzende.
In der Bedeutung „zu" steht „too" vor einem Adjektiv oder Adverb:

> "He is too young to drive a car. His sister drives too fast, too!"

by / buy / bye

Die Schreibweise „bye" findest du nur im Gruß „Bye-bye" oder „Bye" (Tschüss!). Das Verb „buy" (kaufen) und die Präposition „by" (by bus, by the river) wirst du sicher im Zusammenhang unterscheiden können. Schließlich „kauft" man keinen Fluss!

ÜBUNG 2

Jetzt kannst du dein gesammeltes Wissen ausprobieren. Fülle jede Lücke mit einem Wort aus, das genauso ausgesprochen wird wie ein anderes Wort in derselben Zeile. Etwas Detektivarbeit also! Viel Spaß dabei!

a) We had a barbecue *(Grillfest)* last week. I ate ___eight___ sausages!

b) You're too big for ____________ jeans.

c) Bye-bye! I'm going shopping now. I want to ____________ some food.

d) ____________ you like to go for a walk in the wood?

e) Our train leaves in an ____________.

f) ____________ the boy whose dictations are always full of mistakes?

g) She ____________ that her nose is a bit too long.

h) Two pounds is ____________ much ____________ pay for a hamburger!

i) ____________ these words on the right side of your vocabulary notebook.

j) Of course we ____________ about that new café in the High Street.

k) I've got something in my ____________.

l) ____________ bikes are lying on the grass over there.

m) Can you ____________ me? – No. Where are you? – Over here!

ÜBUNG **3**

Wie wär's mit einem kleinen Kreuzworträtsel zu *simple past*-Formen, die die gleiche Aussprache wie bestimmte andere Wörter haben? Die Zeichnungen stellen die gleich klingenden Wörter dar.
Achtung: Bei Nummer 1 und 6 ist es der Infinitiv, der gleich klingt. Für die Lösung brauchst du aber die *simple past*-Form dieser Verben.

1. 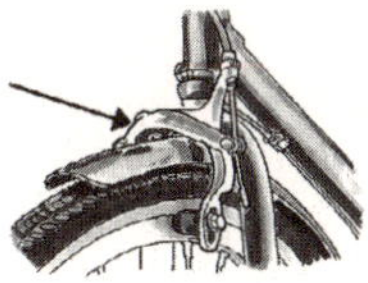

2. 

3. 

4. 

5. 

6. 

7. 

Ähnlich klingende Wörter

Jetzt kommen wir zu Wörtern, die nicht gleich, aber sehr ähnlich ausgesprochen werden. Auch hier lauert die Verwechslungsgefahr! Deshalb kommt jetzt eine kurze Zusammenstellung von Wörtern, die besonders oft verwechselt werden.

ACHTUNG

Ähnliche Aussprache – Nicht verwechseln!

want	–	**won't:**	You won't want to wait, will you?
then	–	**than:**	Then I saw that her ice-cream was bigger than mine.
quite *(ganz)*	–	**quiet:** *(ruhig)*	It was quite quiet in the classroom.
walk	–	**work:**	My father usually walks to work. It's a nice walk.
foot	–	**food:**	I cut my foot on some glass. – I cut my food with a knife.
feed	–	**feet:**	DO NOT FEED THE MONKEYS. – One foot, two feet.

ÜBUNG **4**

Ergänze folgende Sätze mit dem passenden Wort aus dem ACHTUNG-Kästchen. Jedes Wort wird nur *einmal* gebraucht. Bei „walk“ und „work“ kann es sich um ein Verb oder um ein Substantiv handeln.

a) Yesterday we went for a ______________ in the country.

b) It was very ______________ there,

c) and the air was much cleaner ______________ in the town!

d) We had a picnic in the woods and ______________ we went home.

e) On the way home my sister fell and hurt *(to hurt = verletzen)* her ______________.

f) We had to carry her to the bus stop! When we got home, my _____________ hurt, too!

g) But we had a wonderful day. Do you _____________ to come with us next time?

h) "Don't forget to _____________ your hamster!" –

i) "I gave him some _____________ this morning.

j) He looks _____________ happy." –

k) "He _____________ live very long if you don't give him enough to eat!"

l) My parents have good jobs. They _____________ in an office in London.

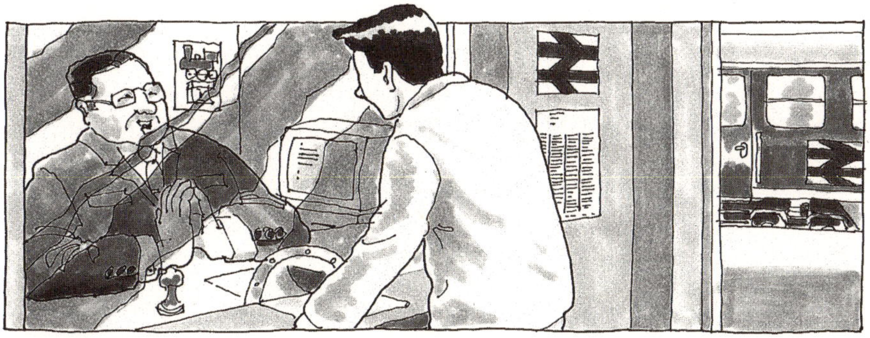

At a railway station:

Passenger:	"Too-too-too-ting!"
Booking clerk (Schalterbeamter):	"What? Are you trying to be funny?"
Passenger:	"No. I want **two** tickets **to Too**ting, please!"

DIKTAT 23

Und jetzt solltest du als Abschluss dieses Kapitels ein kurzes Diktat schreiben. Lass dir den Text diktieren – Diktat Nr. 23.

In dem Diktat kommt ein Inselname vor, den du vielleicht noch nicht kennst:

Lundy Island = britische Insel im Bristolkanal

Merke dir die Schreibweise gut.

„Silent letters“ – Buchstaben, die nicht ausgesprochen werden

9

„Englische Wörter stecken voller Buchstaben, die geschrieben, aber nicht gesprochen werden.“ Diese Meinung teilst du sicher auch. Besonders bei Diktaten kann dieser Umstand verheerende Folgen haben!

REGEL

Beispiele für „silent letters“:

Nicht auszusprechen – wohl aber zu schreiben! – sind folgende „stumme“ Buchstaben:

1. **k** am Wortanfang in der Kombination **kn**

   wie in: knee *(Knie)*, knife, knock *(klopfen)*, know / knew / known

2. **w** in folgenden Fällen:
   am Wortanfang in der Kombination **wr** : write, writer, wrong
   und in den Wörtern sword *(Schwert)*, two, answer

   Zu **w** siehe auch den nächsten Achtung-Kasten!

3. **-b** nach **-m-** in folgenden Wörtern:

   climb (auch nicht in climbing, climber, climbed), thumb *(Daumen)*, comb (*Kamm, kämmen,* auch nicht vor **-ing** und **-ed**)

4. **-gh-** in der Wortmitte oder am Wortende (besonders vor **-t**)

   wie in: light, high, night, right, thought, brought, ought *(sollte)*

   Beachte: Bei den wenigen Wörtern, die mit **gh-** anfangen, werden diese Buchstaben [g] ausgesprochen: **gh**ost *(Gespenst)* usw.

5. **-t-** nach **s** in der Mitte von vielen Wörtern

   wie in: listen, castle, whistle

ACHTUNG

Besonders tückisch ist die Kombination **wh**. Sie enthält nämlich in manchen Wörtern das **w** und in anderen das **h** als „silent letter“!

Beispiele für **w** als „silent letter“: who, whose, whole
Beispiele für **h** als „silent letter“: when, where, why, what, white

ÜBUNG 1

Ein Kreuzworträtsel zu einigen der „stummen“ Buchstaben in der Regelbox. Aufgepasst: Nicht alle Lösungswörter enthalten „silent letters“!

Down *(senkrecht)*

1 

2 This word rhymes with “won”

4 Girls wear these on their legs in winter

5 The opposite of 6 down

6 In Britain we drive on the left, in Germany you drive on the ...

9 You can swim in this

12 The opposite of “off”

Across *(waagerecht)*

1 This word sounds like “no”

3 You need 1 Down to do this

5 He or she writes things

7 The opposite of “low”

8 Three big boys and two small ...

10 You can often find this in 13 Across

11 A hamster is not ... big as a dog

13 Big, old building where a king or prince lives

Merke

Folgende „silent letters“ kommen meist in der Wortmitte oder am Wortende vor:

-l-: wie in: half, talk, walk; could, would, should
-r(-): wie in: or, for, horse, of course *(natürlich)*, her, first

Achtung: Bei der Endung **-r** (teacher, or, her, far usw.) hörst du das **-r** nur, wenn ein Vokal folgt. Du darfst aber nicht vergessen, das **-r** im Diktat zu schreiben!

She is our teacher. (**-r** ist stumm, wird aber geschrieben)	Our teacher_ is good. (**-r** als Übergang hörbar)

ÜBUNG 2

Kennst du die englische Übersetzung dieser zehn deutschen Wörter? Jedes englische Wort enthält mindestens einen „stummen Buchstaben“! Unterstreiche die „silent letters“.

a) Kreide	chalk	f) früh	________
b) arm	________	g) zuhören	________
c) Wann?	________	h) Gabel	________
d) Fluss	________	i) Wer?	________
e) Auto	________	j) brachte	________

ÜBUNG 3

Are you a good detective?

Der folgende kleine Text enthält Wörter mit einem oder mehreren „stummen Buchstaben“. Unterstreiche die „silent letters“.
Achtung: Etliche der gesuchten „stummen Buchstaben“ wurden in diesem Kapitel noch nicht behandelt!

Guess where I went last summer! I stayed with a friend in Northern Germany. She and her family live on a small island – they call it a „Hallig“ – near Husum. It was my first visit to a foreign country and I was very excited. I took a big suitcase and my guitar with me. The train trip from London to Husum took 15 hours! I was very hungry and thirsty when I arrived. I only had a packet of biscuits and two bottles of fruit juice with me! My friend and her family met me at the station. They were waiting under the station sign. Their house is an old building on a small island only two metres above the water!

Trage jetzt die Wörter, welche die folgenden **neuen** stummen Buchstaben enthalten, in die entsprechende Spalte ein. Die „silent letters“ solltest du in einer anderen Farbe hervorheben.

“New” silent letters:

-g-	**-i-**	**-u-**	**-s-**	**h-** (am Wortanfang)	**-e** (am Wortende)
________	________	Guess	________	________	________
________	________	________			________
	________	________			________
	________	________			________
					________
					________
					________

Tipp

Übernimm die Liste aus der letzten Übung in dein Vokabelheft, und zwar unter der Überschrift „silent letters“. Trage auch alle anderen Wörter mit stummen Buchstaben, die in diesem Kapitel genannt werden, in diese Liste ein.
Lass etwas Platz in jeder Spalte für entsprechende Wörter, die du im Laufe der Zeit zusätzlich lernst.

Merke

Checkliste

Es folgen weitere, dir bekannte Wörter, die „silent letters" enthalten, über die du im nächsten Diktat vielleicht stolpern könntest:

Nicht vergessen!

-n am Wortende bei „autumn", „hymn" *(Hymne)*
-u- in „aunt", „Auntie"
-e- in einzelnen Wörtern wie z. B. „interest", „interested", interesting", „different", „foreign" (hier ist auch das **-g-** stumm)

Zu guter Letzt eine Übung, in der „silent letters" ausgelassen wurden.

ÜBUNG 4 Trage die fehlenden „stummen" Buchstaben in die Lücken ein.

a) Can you g_u_ess where my A___nt Rosemary lives?

b) In an old cas___le! She wo___ks there.

c) Don't laugh! It isn't a joke *(Witz)* and she isn't a g___ost!

d) She is a g___ide *(Fremdenführerin)*.

e) She lives in a modern flat in one of the old b___ildings.

f) The cas___le is on a small i___land in the middle of a lake.

g) Visitors come by boat throu___ a gate *(Tor)* in the hi___ wall.

h) My a___nt locks the gate and switches off the li___ts every ni___t.

i) But she is safe enough. No one cou___d clim___ the walls!

j) I ___now you are int___rested in old b___ildings.

k) Wou___d you like to visit this cas__le? Shou___d we go there next week?

ACHTUNG

Keine „silent letters“, aber dennoch eine böse Falle bei Diktaten:

-gh am Ende einiger Wörter wird [f] ausgesprochen.

Beispiele: enough, laugh, tough *(zäh)*, rough *(grob)*, cough *(husten / Husten)*.

Dieses **-gh** darfst du nicht mit dem stummen **-gh** in „through“, „caught“ usw. verwechseln!

DIKTAT 24

Und jetzt solltest du als Abschluss dieses Kapitels ein kurzes Diktat schreiben. Lass dir den Text diktieren – Diktat Nr. 24.

In dem Diktat kommt ein Wort vor, das du vielleicht noch nicht kennst:

place [pleis] = Platz, Stelle

10 Laute und ihre Schreibweisen (I)

Schön wäre es, wenn einem Laut nur *ein* einziger Buchstabe im Alphabet entspräche! Das hieße beim Diktat, dass du nur schreiben müsstest, was du hörst. Leider ist die englische Sprache diesbezüglich nicht so einfach. Besonders bei den **Vokalen** (Selbstlauten) musst du sehr aufpassen: Die Worte „br**o**ther“ und „b**u**tter“ enthalten den gleichen Laut [ʌ], der aber in den beiden Wörtern unterschiedlich geschrieben wird. Dasselbe gilt für den Laut [ɜː] in „b**ir**d“, „h**ear**d“, „w**ere**“ und „w**or**d“.

Diese Unterschiede zwischen Aussprache und Schreibung können für dein nächstes Diktat verheerende Folgen haben. Dem wollen wir in den Kapiteln „Laute und ihre Schreibweisen“ vorbeugen.

In diesem Kapitel beschäftigen wir uns mit den oben als Beispiele genannten Vokalen, also mit dem kurzen Vokal [ʌ] wie z. B. in „b**u**tter“ und dem langen Vokal [ɜː] wie z. B. in „b**ir**d“.

Merke

Die Schreibweisen des Vokals [ʌ]

Typische Schreibweise:

-u- wie in: but, cut, sun, luck

Sonstige Schreibweisen:

-o- besonders vor **-th** wie in:
mother, brother, other, another
sowie in vielen anderen Wörtern:
above, colour, come, front, honey, love, money, month, none, nothing, some(thing), son

-ou- besonders vor **-gh** wie in:
enough, country, courage, cousin, rough *(grob)*, touch, tough *(zäh)*, young

Beachte:
Bei den drei **-ough**-Wörtern wird das **-gh** [f] ausgesprochen.

Sonderfall:

-oe- **nur** in does

ÜBUNG

1 Schreibe die fehlenden Buchstaben in die Lücken. Es handelt sich immer um Schreibweisen des Vokals [ʌ].

a) My little br_o_ther l_o_ves toast with b_u_tter and h_o_ney.

b) D___s your m___ther give you en___gh pocket m___ney *(Taschengeld)*?

c) Mrs Brown's y___ng s___n is sitting in the s___n.

d) My m___m d___sn't want to c___me to the football match.

e) Last m___nth I w___n £100 in the National Lottery.

Trage nun alle Wörter, die einen [ʌ]-Laut enthalten, in die Zeile mit der entsprechenden Schreibweise ein:

f) Schreibweise **u**: ______________________

g) Schreibweise **o**: ______________________

h) Schreibweise **ou**: ______________________

i) Schreibweise **oe**: ______________________

Merke

Die Schreibweisen des Vokals [ɜ:]

Typische Schreibweise:

-er- wie in: German(y), her, term usw.
-ir- wie in: bird, birthday, first, girl usw.
-or- wie in: word, work, world, worse usw.
-ur- wie in: burn, burglar *(Einbrecher)*, excursion *(Ausflug)*, turn usw.

Seltenere Schreibweise:

(-)ear- wie in: earth, early, heard, learn und einigen weiteren Wörtern

ÜBUNG 2

Jedes Wort in diesem kleinen Kreuzworträtsel enthält den Laut [ɜ:]. Kannst du das Rätsel lösen?

1. "Cat" is a … with three letters
2. 
3. My father goes to … every day, except on Saturdays and Sundays.
4. "…, second, third!"
5. 
6. The board you need to ride on the waves *(Wellen)* is called a "… board".
7. Opposite of "him"

Merke

Das Dehnungs -r

Die Buchstaben **a, e, i, o** und **u** werden im Englischen vor **-r** oft gedehnt, d. h. lang ausgesprochen, ohne dass das **-r** selbst ausgesprochen wird (außer manchmal im amerikanischen Englisch).

Vergleiche das Wort „**cat**“ mit „**car**“, „**give**“ mit „**girl**“, „**but**“ mit „**burn**“ usw.

ÜBUNG **3**

Kannst du die Wörter im Kreis in die richtige Spalte einordnen? Aber aufgepasst: Einige Wörter lassen sich – trotz Ähnlichkeiten in der Schreibweise – in keine der beiden Spalten einordnen!

butcher, found, trouble, round, hungry, could, perfect, terrible, sir, beach, push, verb, cup, thirsty, term, cousin, nervous, double, purse, counter, full

[ʌ] wie in „but“	[ɜː] wie in „her“
cup	nervous
______	______
______	______
______	______
______	______
	______
	______

DIKTAT **25**

Und jetzt solltest du als Abschluss dieses Kapitels ein kurzes Diktat schreiben. Lass dir den Text diktieren – Diktat Nr. 25.

11 Die Kurzformen der Hilfsverben

Die englischen Hilfsverben werden in der gesprochenen Sprache meist abgekürzt: So wird z. B.

„I am happy“ zu „I'm happy“,
„You have got it“ zu „You've got it“,
„It is late“ zu „It's late“.

Der weggelassene Buchstabe wird durch einen Apostroph ersetzt. Hier heißt es beim Diktat aufpassen: Der Apostroph darf nicht fehlen! Außerdem gibt es Verwechslungsmöglichkeiten mit anderen gleich – oder fast gleich – lautenden Wörtern.

REGEL

Wann dürfen Kurzformen verwendet werden?

Die Kurzformen der Hilfsverben werden in der **gesprochenen** Sprache verwendet. Sie dürfen gebraucht werden nach

Personalpronomen: I'm, you're, he's ...,
that: "That's my bike!",
here und **there**: "Here's my seat and there's your seat.",
einigen **Fragewörtern**: "What's the matter? Where've you been so long? Who's that boy?",
Substantiven: "My mother's been ill.",
Namen: "Tom's my friend.".

REGEL

1. Die Kurzformen des Hilfsverbs „to be“:

bejahte Langform:	**bejahte Kurzform:**	**verneinte Kurzform:**
I am learning English.	“I'm learning English.	I'm not learning French.”
You are my friend.	“You're my friend.	You aren't my sister.”
Ian is coming to my party.	“Ian's coming to my party	but Peter isn't coming.”
The cat is in the kitchen.	“The cat's in the kitchen	but the dog isn't”

Dieselben Kurzformen gelten für **he / she / it is, we / they are.**

2. Die Kurzformen des Hilfsverbs „to have“:

bejahte Langform:	**bejahte Kurzform:**	**verneinte Kurzform:**
I have got a dog.	“I've got a dog	but I haven't got a cat.”
She has got a brother.	“She's got a brother	but she hasn't got a sister.”
My dad has got a bike.	“My dad's got a bike	but my mum hasn't got one.”

Dieselben Kurzformen gelten für **he / it has, we / you / they have.**

Aufgepasst: Die Abkürzung **-'s** kann für **is** und **has** stehen!

He's (= is) driving to Paris today. I hope he'll manage it because he's (= has) got my car!

ÜBUNG **1** Kürze die Hilfsverben in folgenden Sätzen entsprechend ab:

a) I am learning English at school.

“I'm learning English at school. ”

b) We have got a good teacher.

“ ”

c) She is English, but her husband is German.

“ ____ ”

d) They have got two daughters, Penny and Tanya.

“ ____ ”

e) They have not got a son.

“ ____ ”

f) Penny is in my class at school.

“ ____ ”

g) She is not very good at English.

“ ____ ”

h) But her mother is a very good teacher.

“ ____ ”

i) What is your English teacher like?

“ ____ ”

REGEL

Kurzformen von weiteren Hilfsverben

bejahte Langform:	**bejahte Kurzform:**	**verneinte Kurzform:**
I / we / you / they do	–	I / we / you / they don't
he / she / it does	–	he / she / it doesn't
did	–	didn't
can	–	can't
could	–	couldn't
must *(müssen)*	–	mustn't *(nicht dürfen)*
need *(brauchen)*	–	needn't *(nicht müssen)*
will	'll	won't

ÜBUNG 2 Schreibe die Langformen der Hilfsverben auf.

a) "My mother's got a good job.

My mother has got a good job.

b) She's a truck-driver!

c) Don't laugh! It's true *(wahr)*!

d) My father's got a small haulage company *(Spedition)*.

e) My dad's always very busy.

f) He can't do all the work himself.

g) Mum's job's very interesting.

h) It won't be easy for her to do all the housework without help."

ACHTUNG

Folgende abgekürzte Hilfsverben können mit anderen Wörtern verwechselt werden:

1. Gleiche Aussprache – besondere Vorsicht ist geboten!

Langform:	**Kurzform:**	**Verwechslungsmöglichkeit:**	**Beispiel:**
you are	you're	your *(dein, Ihr)*	You're in your room.
it is / it has	it's	its *(sein)*	It's in its box.
who is / who has	who's	whose *(wessen)*	Who's in whose room?
they are	they're	their *(ihr)*	They're in their car.
		there *(dort)*	They're not there.

2. Fast gleiche Aussprache

he is / he has	he's	his *(sein)*	He's with his brother.
we are	we're	were *(war, waren)* where *(wo)*	We're where we were last year!
will not	won't	want *(wollen)*	She won't want to come.

ÜBUNG 3

Vervollständige die Lücken im Dialog mit dem richtigen Wort aus dem Kasten. Vergiss die vielen Verwechslungsmöglichkeiten im Englischen nicht!

were – we're – where   he's – his   want – won't
who's – whose   its – it's   you're – your   their – they're – there

a) "What are you doing this afternoon?" – "We're going swimming.

b) Do you want to come with us?" – "No, I __________ have time.

c) __________ were you yesterday?" – "We __________ at school."

d) "Is Jennifer in your class at school?" – "__________ Jennifer?"

e) "My best friend. Don't you know her?" – "Is she the girl _________ brother works at the garage?"

f) "I think so. But _________ much older than _________ sister.

g) They live in your street." – "Oh, I know! _________ house is on the corner."

h) "That's right. _________ a big house with _________ own swimming pool in the garden! _________ a rich family.

i) I'm going to visit her tomorrow. Can you come, too?" – "Sorry, I _________ to go shopping after school tomorrow."

j) "Well, I hope _________ not too busy to come to my birthday party next week!"

k) "Is it _________ birthday next week? A party? I'd love to come!"

DIKTAT 26

Und jetzt solltest du als Abschluss dieses Kapitels ein kurzes Diktat schreiben. Lass dir den Text diktieren – Diktat Nr. 26.

In dem Diktat kommt ein Wort vor, das du vielleicht noch nicht kennst:

fireworks = Feuerwerk, Feuerwerkskörper

Merke dir die Schreibweise dieses Wortes gut.

12 Laute und ihre Schreibweisen (II)

Nehmen wir mal an, du bekommst Folgendes diktiert:

"What has he got in his hand? – A sausage."

Im Diktat hörst du die fett gedruckten Buchstaben jeweils als Selbstlaut [ɒ]. Geschrieben wird dieser Laut jedoch in unserem Beispielsatz auf drei verschiedene Arten – eine große Fehlerquelle bei Diktaten!

In diesem Kapitel werden wir auf die Schreibweisen des oben genannten kurzen Vokals [ɒ] sowie auf die Schreibweisen der beiden langen Vokale [ɑ:] wie z. B. in „car" und „last" und [ɔ:] wie z. B. in „small" und „door" eingehen.

Merke

Die Schreibweisen des Vokals [ɒ]

Typische Schreibweise:

-o- wie in: got, hot, stop, pot, of, off, on

und bei fast allen kurzen Wörtern, die diesen Buchstaben als einzigen Vokal enthalten.
Aber nicht in kurzen Wörtern mit **-re** oder **-r** am Ende:
mo**re**, sto**re**, o**r**, fo**r** usw.
Durch diese Endungen wird der Vokal gedehnt, also lang ausgesprochen (siehe Schreibweisen des Vokals [ɔ:], S. 194).

Sonstige Schreibweisen:

-a- wie in: want, what, watch, halt *(= anhalten)*, salt
-au- wie in: Austria(n), Australia(n), sausage *(= Wurst, Würstchen)*

ÜBUNG **1**

Schreibe die fehlenden Buchstaben in die Lücken. Es handelt sich immer um eine mögliche Schreibweise des Vokals [ɒ].

a) It is often very h_o_t. in _Au_stralia.

b) You've g__t a l__t of CDs.
I w__nt to see them.

c) I bought these s__sages at the butcher's sh__p.

d) "Wh__t's wr__ng?" – "I forg__t to put __n my w__tch this morning!"

e) Alois is fr__m Innsbruck.
He's an __strian.

Trage nun alle Wörter, die einen [ɒ]-Laut enthalten, in die Zeile mit der entsprechenden Schreibweise ein:

f) Schreibweise **o**: hot, ______________________________

g) Schreibweise **a**: ______________________________

h) Schreibweise **au**: ______________________________

Schauen wir uns nun die Schreibweisen der wichtigsten dir bisher bekannten Wörter mit dem langen Vokal [ɑː] wie in „car" an.

Merke

Die Schreibweisen des Vokals [ɑː]

Typische Schreibweise:

-ar(-) wie in: art, car, far, party, star, start

Sonstige Schreibweisen:

-a- hauptsächlich in: father, dance, glass, last, past, path oder vor **-lf** in: half, calf

-au- in ganz wenigen Wörtern wie: laugh, aunt

-ea- in: heart *(= Herz)*

ÜBUNG **2**

Streiche die Wörter durch, die *nicht* den Vokal [ɑ:] enthalten. Achtung: Es kann sich um mehr als ein Wort in jeder Reihe handeln!

a) far – cat – postcard – Carol – park – dark

b) hard – happy – caravan – daughter – half – laugh

c) aunt – Australia – laugh – caught – part – heart

Merke

Die Schreibweisen des Vokals [ɔ:]

Typische Schreibweise:

-or wie in: or, cornflakes, for, important, forty
-ore in kurzen Wörtern wie more, score, store, wore
-oor wie in: door, floor und einigen wenigen Wörtern

Sonstige Schreibweisen:

-a- vor **-l-** wie in: all, always, ball, call, fall, small, talk, walk

Beachte: Bei **half** und **calf** wird das **a** jedoch [ɑ:] ausgesprochen (siehe Schreibweisen des Vokals [ɑ:]).

-ar- in: warm, war *(= Krieg)* und einigen wenigen Wörtern
-aw wie in: saw, draw, law *(= Gesetz)*, paw *(= Pfote)*
-au- (besonders vor **-ght**): daughter, taught, caught, fault *(= Fehler)* usw.
-ou- (besonders vor **-ght**): bought, brought, thought, four, of course
-a- (selten) wie in: water

ÜBUNG 3

Schreibe aus der folgenden Liste alle Wörter ab, die den Vokal [ɔ:] enthalten. Wie viele sind es insgesamt?

port – door – too – saw – bought – stop – fourteen – flower – warm – farm – hall – story – hard – water – daughter – laugh – thought – wall

[ɔ:]: ______________________________

____

ÜBUNG 4

Alle diese Wörter enthalten einen [ɑ:]-, [ɔ:]- oder [ɒ]-Laut. Mal sehen, ob du die Wörter in die richtige Spalte einordnen kannst!

sport hard fault forest warm what ball class pass strawberry shock bar fork

[ɑ:] wie in „car“,	[ɔ:] wie in „for“	[ɒ] wie in „hot“
hard	______	______
______	______	______
______	______	______
______	______	
	______	
	______	

DIKTAT 27

Und jetzt solltest du als Abschluss dieses Kapitels ein kurzes Diktat schreiben. Lass dir den Text diktieren – Diktat Nr. 27.

13 Zusammensetzungen: Bindestrich? Zwei Worte? Ein Wort?

Nichts ist uneinheitlicher als die Verwendung des Bindestrichs im Englischen. Warum schreibt man z. B. „bedroom" zusammen, „living-room" aber mal mit Bindestrich, mal als zwei Worte? Keiner weiß genau warum. Deshalb gibt es keine exakten Regeln, die alle Fälle abdecken.

Du solltest aber wenigstens die Fälle kennen, in denen ein fehlender (oder überflüssiger) Bindestrich bzw. „zwei Worte statt einem Wort" im Diktat als halber Fehler gelten.

Bindestrich

REGEL

Ein Bindestrich wird **immer** benutzt:

1. bei den Grundzahlen von 21 bis 99:
   My father is thirty-five and my grandmother is sixty-one.

2. bei den Ordnungszahlen von 21. bis 99.:
   Today is my uncle's thirty-third birthday.

3. bei zusammengesetzten Adjektiven (zwei oder mehr Worte, besonders in Zusammenhang mit Zahlwörtern):
   "We walked five miles." – "What? You went for a five-mile walk!"

ÜBUNG 1

... 30th ... 31st ... 32nd ... 33rd ... 34th ... 35th ...

Der große Volksmarathon ist fast vorbei, aber nicht nur die ersten drei Sieger werden geehrt: Jeder Läufer erhält eine Rangnummer. Trage die fehlenden Zahlwörter in die Rangliste ein:

a) Number twenty-four came thirtieth.

b) Number ______________ came ____________________.

c) Number ______________ came ____________________.

d) Number ______________ came ____________________.

e) Number ______________ came ____________________.

f) Number ______________ came ____________________.

ACHTUNG

Die Ordnungszahlen: Besonderheiten in der Rechtschreibung

1. Bei den Zehnerzahlen von 20–90 wird **-y** vor **-th** in **-ie** umgewandelt:

Beispiele:	twenty (20)	–	twentieth (20.)
	thirty (30)	–	thirtieth (30.)
	ninety (90)	–	ninetieth (90.)
Vergleiche:	Auch vor der Endung **-s** wird **-y** zu **-ie**, sofern vor dem **-y** ein Konsonant steht:		
	to hurry	–	she hurries
	one baby	–	two babies

2. Beachte weiterhin folgende Unterschiede in der Schreibung:

five (5)	–	fifth (5.)
eight (8)	–	eighth (8.)
nine (9)	–	ninth (9.)
twelve (12)	–	twelfth (12.)

Ein Wort oder zwei Worte?

Allgemein kann man sagen, dass Wörter, die aus zwei Bestandteilen zusammengesetzt werden (z. B. „news“ = Nachrichten + „paper“ = Papier), als **ein** Wort geschrieben werden, wenn sie eine **unabhängige Eigenbedeutung** erhalten: „newspaper“ heißt „Zeitung“ und nicht „Nachrichten-Papier“; „already“ heißt „schon, bereits“ – „We're all ready“ heißt „Wir sind alle bereit“.

Die meisten dieser Worte lernst du als „Ein-Wort-Wörter“. Schreibst du z. B. „already“ öfter im Diktat falsch, dann heißt das einfach: die Vokabeln richtig lernen. Hierfür gibt es keine Rechtschreibregeln.

ÜBUNG 2

Ergänze die Sätze mit „no / some / any / al / all“. Einige dieser „Wortpaare“ werden zusammengeschrieben, andere als zwei Worte. Lass im letzteren Fall einen großzügigen Wortzwischenraum!

NO SOME ANY
AL ALL

a) “Listen! I think I can hear __some__body upstairs in the bedroom.”

b) “But there’s ________body else in the house. We’re alone.

c) I can’t hear ________thing.”

d) “I ________times hear things at night, too.”

e) “Don’t worry. There’s ________thing to worry about. I’m here with you.”

f) “I’m hungry. Have we got ________thing to eat?”

g) “There are ________things in the fridge. Let’s have a look. Are you thirsty?”

h) “No. I’ve ________ready had three glasses of Coke.”

i) “Look. Mum has made us some sandwiches. They’re ________ready to eat.”

j) “That’s ________right, then! Let’s eat!

k) Mum and Dad will be back at ten o’ clock ________way.”

Kontrolliere deine Lösungen und trage dann die Wörter richtig in den folgenden Kasten ein. Diese Auflistung dient dir bei Diktaten als Merkzettel.

Merkzettel

Diese „Wortpaare" schreibe ich zusammen:	Diese „Wortpaare" schreibe ich auseinander:
____________________	____________________
____________________	____________________
____________________	____________________
____________________	
____________________	
____________________	
____________________	

Merke

Wenn du beim Diktat genau zuhörst, stellst du fest, dass viele der „Ein-Wort-Wörter", die du vielleicht als zwei Worte falsch schreiben könntest, nur **eine Hauptbetonung** haben. Sie werden wie ein Wort ausgesprochen und auch so geschrieben (' = die folgende Silbe trägt die Hauptbetonung):

Vergleiche:
al'ready mit 'all 'ready
'sometimes mit 'some 'time
'anything mit 'any 'things usw.

DIKTAT 28

Und jetzt solltest du als Abschluss dieses Kapitels ein kurzes Diktat schreiben. Lass dir den Text diktieren – Diktat Nr. 28.

In dem Diktat kommen zwei Begriffe vor, die dir vielleicht noch unbekannt sind:

gentlemen = meine Herren (in der Anrede)
Birmingham = Stadt in Mittelengland

Präge dir die Schreibweise dieser Wörter ein.

14 Laute und ihre Schreibweisen (III)

In unserem letzten Kapitel, das sich mit den unterschiedlichen Schreibweisen von Lauten beschäftigt, geht es um folgende Selbstlaute:

dem kurzen Vokal [ʊ] wie z. B. in „**book**“, „**could**“ oder „**push**“,
dem langen Vokal [u:] wie z. B. in „**school**“, „**group**“ oder „**whose**“ und
dem langen Vokal [i:] wie z. B. in „**feed**“, „**thief**“ oder „**easy**“.

Merke

Die Schreibweisen des Vokals [ʊ]

Häufige Schreibweisen:

-u- wie in: butcher, full, pull, pullover, push, put
-oo- wie in: foot, good, look, book, took
-ou- in den Hilfsverben could, would, should

Seltene Schreibweise:

-o- wie in: woman

Die Schreibweise **u** für den kurzen Laut [ʌ] in „b**u**t“, „sh**u**t“ usw. hast du in Kapitel 10 geübt. Die folgende Übung zeigt dir, ob du die unterschiedlichen Schreibweisen des Vokals [ʊ] (wie z. B. in „p**u**t“ und „b**oo**k“) sowie die gleiche Schreibweise der Vokale [ʌ] und [ʊ] (wie z. B. bei „sh**u**t“ = [ʌ] und „p**u**t“ = [ʊ]) auseinander halten kannst!

ÜBUNG 1

Schreibe die fehlenden Buchstaben in die Lücken. Es handelt sich entweder um eine Schreibweise des Vokals [ʊ] oder um eine Schreibweise des Vokals [ʌ]. Trage anschließend die Wörter in die entsprechende Spalte neben dem Dialog ein.

		[ʊ] wie in „pull“	[ʌ] wie in „but“
a) *Mother:*	J<u>u</u>st l__k at your room, Jason!	________	Just
b)	Pick __p your b__ks and	________	________
c)	p__t them in your c__pboard!	________	________
d) *Jason:*	B__t it's already f__ll, M__m!	________	________
e) *Mother:*	Well, w__ld you p__t them	________	________
	__nder your bed, please?	________	________

Alles richtig? Falls du Probleme mit den Schreibweisen des Vokals [ʌ] hattest, schau dir noch mal Kapitel 10 an.

Den Doppelbuchstaben **oo** hast du gerade als eine Schreibweise für den kurzen Vokal [ʊ] kennen gelernt, z. B. in „**look**“. Noch häufiger ist **oo** jedoch eine der Schreibweisen für den langen Vokal [u:].

Merke

Schreibweisen des Vokals [u:]

Schreibweisen als Doppelbuchstabe:

-oo- wie in: choose, cool, food, school, too, tool, tooth *(= Zahn)*
-ou- wie in: you, soup, group
-ue- wie in: blue, true
-ew- wie in: crew, threw

Seltener:

-ui- in: fruit, juice, suitcase
-oe- in: shoe
-wo- in: two
-ou- in: through

Schreibweisen als Einzelbuchstabe:

-o- in den kurzen Wörtern do, who, whose sowie in Wörtern mit einem stummen End-**e** und ihren Ableitungen: lose, loser *(= Verlierer)*, move, moving-van *(= Möbelwagen)* usw.

-u- wie in: rule *(= Regel)*, ruler

ÜBUNG **2**

Die fehlenden Buchstaben in dieser Übung sind lauter **o** – aber handelt es sich um Einzel-**o** oder Doppel-**o**? Fülle die Lücken aus.

a) I'm l*oo*king for a b___k about Indian c___king.

b) Wh___'s that w___man over there? –

c) I can see three w___men. D___ you mean the one in the ___range dress?

d) Shut the d___r and sit down on the fl___r.

e) He is m___re interested in his h___bbies than in his sch___l work.

f) D___ you like French, t___?

g) The ___pposite of "rich" is "poor".

h) The f___d is very g___d.

Prüfe dein Ergebnis und trage die Wörter in der entsprechenden Spalte der folgenden Liste ein. Die Liste dient dir als kleiner Merkzettel, den du nochmals durchlesen solltest, bevor du das Diktat zu diesem Kapitel schreibst. Er wird dir gute Dienste leisten!

Schreibweise -oo-			**Schreibweise -o-**		
[ʊ] wie in „**look**" (kurz)	[u:] wie in „**too**" (lang)	[ɔ:] wie in „**or**" (lang)	[ɒ] wie in „**of**" (kurz)	[u:] wie in „**too**" (lang)	[ɔ:] wie in „**or**" (lang)
looking	___	___	___	___	___
___	___	___	___	___	
___	___		___	___	
___					

Welche Wörter konntest du *nicht* einordnen? Es sind die Wörter

___________ und ___________. Merke dir die Schreibweise dieser Wörter

besonders gut!

ACHTUNG

Bei den Wörtern

few, kn**ew**, n**ew**, n**ew**s, **new**spaper, b**eau**ty *(= Schönheit)*, b**eau**tiful usw.

hört man vor dem langen Vokal den Laut [j] wie in „**y**ou". Der Laut [j] wird aber **nicht geschrieben**!

Als letzten Vokal schauen wir uns nun die unterschiedlichen Schreibweisen für den langen Vokal [i:] wie z. B. in „feet" und „easy" an.

Merke

Schreibweisen des Vokals [i:]

Schreibweisen als Doppelbuchstabe:

-ee- wie in: been *(= gewesen)*, feet, freeze, meet, tree

-ea- wie in: beach, bean *(= Bohne)*, clean, each, easy, lead, mean, meat

-ie- wie in: piece, believe, field, niece *(= Nichte)*, thief *(= Dieb)*

Seltener:

-ei- in: receive *(= empfangen)*, receiver *(= Empfänger; Telefonhörer)*

-eo- in: people

Schreibweisen als Einzelbuchstabe:

e- am Wortanfang wie in: even, equal

-e am Wortende wie in: be, he, me, she, we

-e- vor einem stummen End-**e** wie in: complete

Ganz selten:

-i- wie in: police, ski

ÜBUNG 3

Die Aussprache der ausgelassenen Einzel- oder Doppelbuchstaben ist immer [i:]. Kannst du die Wörter richtig ergänzen?

a) H__ asked m__ to m__t him at thr__ o'clock.

b) W__ can have a cup of t__ or coff__ on the b__ch.

c) PL__SE DO NOT PUT YOUR F__T ON THE S__TS

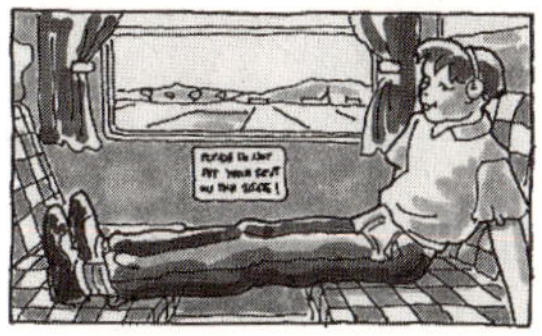

d) I had a p__ce of cake after my m__l.

e) Too many sw__ts are bad for your t__th.

f) Our English t__cher lives in our str__t.

g) The pol__ce were here last w__k.

h) Sh__ doesn't __t m__t or ch__se.

i) W__ n__dn't wait for the other p__ple.

j) He picked up the telephone rec__ver and rang his n__ce up.

k) Pl__se compl__te th__se sentences.

ÜBUNG 4

Nicht alle Wörter, die mit **ea** geschrieben werden, spricht man mit langem i aus. Schreibe das Wort, das nicht in die Reihe passt, daneben.

a) east – mean – meal – breakfast ____________

b) teacher – seat – head – east ____________

c) heavy – cheap – clean – easy ____________

d) at least – ready – beach – dream ____________

ACHTUNG

Verwechsle nicht **the sea** (das Meer) und **to see** (sehen)! (Diese beiden Wörter sind Homonyme, d. h. Wörter, die gleich ausgesprochen, aber verschieden geschrieben werden.

ÜBUNG 5

Ergänze die Wörter.

a) Can you s____ Kate?

b) Yes, she's swimming in the s____.

c) The s____ must be cold today, you can s____ that Kate's skin is blue.

ACHTUNG

Im Englischen ist ein Doppelbuchstabe oft ein Zeichen dafür, dass aus einem kurzen Vokal ein langer Vokal wird:

dog [dɒg] – **door** [dɔ:], **met** [met] – **meet** [mi:t].

Die Buchstaben **a**, **i** und **u** werden im Englischen selten verdoppelt. Kommen also in deinem Diktat Wörter mit **aa**, **ii** (außer „sk**ii**ng") oder **uu** vor, so hast du jeweils einen Fehler gemacht!

ÜBUNG 6

Jetzt kannst du den Lehrer spielen! Ein Klassenkamerad bittet um Hilfe, und du diktierst ihm einige kurze Sätze. Aber in jedem Satz ist ein Rechtschreibfehler. Findest du sie alle? Schreibe die richtige Form des Wortes auf die Zeile neben jeden Satz.

a) My faather has a new car. ____father____

b) I like sking. ____________

c) We sat down on the flur. ____________

d) We went too the cinema yesterday. ____________

e) The children are liing on the beach. ____________

f) Open the dor, please. ____________

Hier noch ein wichtiger Hinweis als Hilfestellung für dein Diktat:

ACHTUNG

Achte besonders auf den Endkonsonanten bei verwechslungsträchtigen Wortpaaren wie:

feet (stimmlos) – feed (stimmhaft)
foot (stimmlos) – food (stimmhaft – außerdem langer Vokal)
got (stimmlos) – God *(= Gott)* (stimmhaft)
dock (stimmlos) – dog (stimmhaft)

und viele andere mehr! Leg dir eine Liste im Vokabelheft an!

ÜBUNG 7

Unregelmäßige Mehrzahlformen

In diesem Kapitel bist du den unregelmäßigen Pluralformen „women“ und „feet“ begegnet. Zum Abschluss wollen wir mit einem Kreuzworträtsel mal testen, ob du alle dir bisher bekannten unregelmäßigen Mehrzahlformen beherrschst. Gefragt wird nach *Singular-* und nach *Pluralformen*.

1 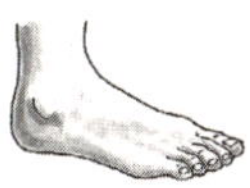
2 
3 
4 

			1		2			3			4
		5									
	6										
7											
				8							

5 
6 
7 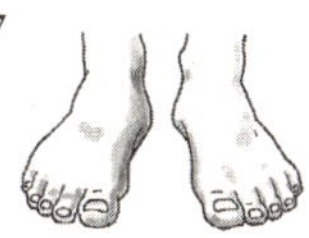
8 

29
30
31

Zu diesem schwierigen Kapitel kannst du drei Diktate schreiben: Nr. 29, 30 und 31.

In Diktat Nr. 29 kommt ein Straßenname vor, den du vielleicht nicht kennst:

York Road

DIKTATE

DIKTAT

1 The Parkers in town

The Parkers live in a small village ten miles from the next town. This Saturday they are in town. Tom must have new shoes, and Molly, his little sister, must have new jeans.
Tom wants black shoes and Molly wants white jeans. And chips with ketchup at McDonald's!
The Parkers go to town in their car. In town, there are a lot of cars, vans, lorries and buses. Where can they park the car? There is a big car park at McDonald's, but they must buy the clothes for the children first. Mr Parker parks the car in front of the church.
In the centre of the town there are a lot of shops. They buy shiny black shoes for Tom and tight white jeans for Molly.
Now they are all hungry, so they go to McDonald's – hamburgers for Mr and Mrs Parker and Tom and chips with ketchup for Molly. Molly has her new white jeans on. She wants more ketchup on her chips. She opens the ketchup bottle and shakes some ketchup onto her chips. Oh dear! Now there is ketchup on her new white jeans, too!

Verbesserungen:

So schreibe ich die Wörter richtig:

____

____

____

____

____

____

____

____

DIKTAT

2 The Bennetts and the Johnsons

Here are two English families, the Bennetts and the Johnsons. The Bennetts are taxi drivers. They have got two taxis. Mr Bennett's taxi is blue, Mrs Bennett's taxi is black. They have got two sons. Ronny Bennett is nearly eleven, his little brother is three. What is his brother's name? It is Timmy. Ronny and Timmy are good friends.

The Johnsons live near the Bennetts. They have got a boy and a girl. Their names are Kevin and Kate. Is Kevin's sister a nice girl? Well, sometimes she is. Ronny and Kevin are in the same class, they are good friends. They often play football together. Is Kate Ronny's friend, too? No, she isn't. Kate's friends are girls and Blackie, her horse. For Kate, boys are terrible, they have no idea about horses, they can only play football.

Verbesserungen:

So schreibe ich die Wörter richtig:

DIKTAT

3 Mr Parker's birthday

Today is Mr Parker's birthday. Mrs Parker's and the children's birthday presents are lying on the breakfast table. Only Betty's present is not there, she cannot find it.
Mrs Parker's present is a shirt and a tie. The shirt has got white and green stripes, and the tie is brown and yellow.
Molly's present is a drawing of the Parkers' dog. It is a bit difficult to see that it is a dog. Her brother Tom says it looks like two balloons, a big one and a small one on four sticks. Mr Parker says Tom is wrong. It really is Bonzo. Everybody can see that.
Betty is very unhappy, she cannot find the present for her father. It is a drawing of her parents' house.
But where is the drawing? Betty looks for it in her school bag, in her cupboard and under her bed.

She goes back into the living-room. Betty's rabbit is sitting on the sofa. She is sitting on Betty's drawing, but she is not heavy, so the drawing is all right. Betty is happy again. She can give her father his birthday present.

Verbesserungen:

So schreibe ich die Wörter richtig:

DIKTAT

4 New neighbours

We've got new neighbours. A family of five has moved into the house next door. They are Indians and their family name is Singh: S - i - n - g - h. But the children's names are English. The Singhs have three children: two girls and a boy. The girls' names are Anna and Susan. The boy's name is Kim. Kim is in my class. Yesterday I asked him about his parents' jobs. His father's a shop assistant in a men's clothes shop and his mother's a children's doctor. Mrs Singh's surgery is in the High Street. The Singhs' oldest daughter Anna is seventeen. She works in a factory for women's clothes. Kim's hobbies are football and computer games. His younger sister's in my sister's class.

Verbesserungen:

So schreibe ich die Wörter richtig:

DIKTAT

5 Tom and the water-pistol

(Mrs Smith:)	Good morning, boys and girls. I'm your new English teacher. My name is Mrs Smith. Where's the register, please? Oh, here it is. Where's Christine? Isn't she here today? Where is she? Is she ill?
(Tom:)	Yes, she's ill. She's in bed.
(Mrs Smith:)	And where's Ben?
(Tom:)	He's late again. He's often late.
(Mrs Smith:)	Let's start. Oh, Tom! What's that under your English book? Is it a water-pistol?
(Tom:)	There's no water in it, so it isn't a water-pistol, it's just a pistol, Mrs Smith.
(Mrs Smith:)	Tom, no pistols and no water-pistols in class!
(Tom:)	Sorry, Mrs Smith.

Verbesserungen:

So schreibe ich die Wörter richtig:

____

____

____

____

____

____

____

____

DIKTAT

6 In class

It is eight o'clock. The teacher and the pupils are in class:

Good morning, girls and boys. Sit down, please. Can you open the window, please, John? Have you got your biros and pencils? Have you got your pens, too? Oh, Kevin hasn't got his pen. Who's got a pen for Kevin? Ronny, look, your exercise book is on the floor. Helen, put your school-bag under your desk. Tom and Christine aren't here today. Tom is ill, he's got a cold. Where's Ben? He's late again, of course!

Counting rhyme

One, two,
where's my shoe?
Three, four,
behind the door.
One, three,
come with me.
Two, four,
shut the door.
Four, two,
you're out, too.

Verbesserungen:

So schreibe ich die Wörter richtig:

____

____

____

____

____

____

DIKTAT

7 Molly Parker and her kitten

Molly likes kittens very much, but there are no cats or kittens on her father's farm.
Almost every day she talks about her friends' pets. Why can't she have a little kitten? Tomorrow is her birthday.
The next afternoon Mr Parker comes home early. He is carrying a box with holes in it. Molly is waiting for him at the door. She opens the box. There is a nice little kitten in it. A white kitten with two black feet and one black ear.
Molly calls her Miss Kitty White. She takes her kitten out into the garden. Look! There is a mouse coming out of a hole in the ground. The kitten jumps out of the box and runs up to the hole. The ground is wet and dirty. She is pushing her head into the hole, but she cannot catch the mouse.
Now look at the kitten! She is not black and white now, she is black and brown. Tom is laughing and Molly, too. She takes Miss Kitty Brown into the bathroom and washes her.

Verbesserungen:

So schreibe ich die Wörter richtig:

____

____

____

____

____

____

____

____

____

DIKTAT

8 What they do at work and in their free time

Every day Mr Bennett collects passengers in his taxi and takes them to different places, for example to the station. If they have got heavy bags and suitcases, he carries them to the platform.
Miss Smith is a teacher. She teaches English and Maths at London Road School. She has a young son, Peter. Peter is four years old.
Every morning she drives Peter to play-school. Peter stays at play-school all day, and his mother fetches him in the afternoon. Then she starts her second job – housewife and mother. She makes dinner while Peter plays in the garden. After dinner she washes Peter and puts him to bed. Life is not easy for a single parent.
Mike Brown is a student. In his holidays he tries to earn some money, but it is not easy to find a part-time job. This summer he is washing dishes in a restaurant for £ 5 an hour. Not a lot of money, but Mike is happy to have a job.
Kevin usually does his homework from half past four to half past five. After that he plays computer games or watches TV. He goes to bed at ten o'clock.

Verbesserungen:

So schreibe ich die Wörter richtig:

DIKTAT

9 Late for work again?

Penny Robinson works in an office. In summer she cycles to work. But in winter she goes by bus. She usually catches the 8.15 bus. Penny always tries to get up early, but today she is late. The bus is leaving in ten minutes! She is tying her shoes, brushing her hair and putting her things into her bag at the same time. Now she is running to the bus stop. Now she is on the bus. Penny buys a ticket and sits down. Why is the bus so empty today? Then she suddenly remembers. Today is Saturday!

Verbesserungen:

So schreibe ich die Wörter richtig:

DIKTAT

10 Happy holidays

This year school started on September 3rd. In the first lesson the boys and girls talked about their summer holidays. Alan visited Germany. He stayed with a family in a small village near Heidelberg. One afternoon he cycled to Heidelberg with his friend Wolfgang. Alan wanted to see the River Neckar. The two boys stopped on a bridge across the river. They watched the big boats on the river for about an hour. Then they dropped sticks into the water and tried to hit them with small stones. After that they played football with some boys and girls in a small park. At seven o'clock they cycled back. They arrived home at a quarter to eight.

Verbesserungen:

So schreibe ich die Wörter richtig:

DIKTAT

11 An afternoon at the farm

Last week I read about a farm open-day in the newspaper. My sister knew where the farm was so we cycled there on Saturday afternoon. We left home after lunch. I took my camera with me. We cycled out into the country and turned off the main road after about four miles. A small road led to the farm. We saw lots of people there, and there were lots of things to do. We fed the horses and threw old bread to the ducks on the pond. We bought some cakes, sat down on the grass and ate them. We drank some fresh milk. My sister rode one of the ponies. I held the pony's head and another boy took a photo of us. We thought it was a wonderful afternoon.

Verbesserungen:

So schreibe ich die Wörter richtig:

DIKTAT

12 A walk in the park

Sandra was in the park with her dog Robin yesterday. Robin is big, but suddenly a bigger dog ran up to them. It was Mr Smith's dog Blacky (*oder:* Blackie), the largest dog in Sandra's street. The two dogs are good friends. Sandra threw a stick and the two dogs ran after it. Blacky was faster than Robin. She fetched the stick most of the time. Then Mr Smith came and went home with Blacky. It was a hot day, the hottest day of the week. Robin is fatter than Blacky, and soon he was the thirstiest dog in the park. There is a lake in the middle of the park. Sandra and Robin walked to the lake. Robin drank some water. Then he jumped into the water. He was happier now.

Verbesserungen:

So schreibe ich die Wörter richtig:

DIKTAT 13

New balls for old

John and Philip were playing football happily in the street. They could play safely in this street. It was a play street in a quiet part of town. There were only a few cars, and they drove very slowly and carefully. The boys usually played football after school. Just when John kicked the ball high in the air, a big car with two young ladies came round the corner. The ball landed in front of the car. The driver stopped quickly, but the car couldn't possibly stop. It drove heavily over the football. Philip shouted angrily. The driver got out and said she was terribly sorry. She gave the boys some money for a new ball. The boys were really happy. It was a very old football.

Verbesserungen:

So schreibe ich die Wörter richtig:

DIKTAT

14 Monday morning

This is the Parker family. Mr Parker is a farmer, Mrs Parker is a teacher. Tom is a pupil at London Road School. His sister Betty is nine and his little sister Molly is two.

It is Monday morning. Time for work and school. Where are Mr Parker's boots? They are not here. And Mrs Parker's shoes? They are not here. Where are they? Where are Tom's exercise books and Betty's school books? They are not in their school bags.

Father looks into Molly's room. Oh look, his boots, Mother's shoes, Tom's exercise books and Betty's school books are under Molly's bed.

Verbesserungen:

So schreibe ich die Wörter richtig:

DIKTAT

15 Ronny and the German test

It is Monday morning. Ronny is still in bed. The alarm clock is ringing.
Oh dear, it is eight o'clock. School starts at a quarter to nine. The first lesson is German, and there is a German test tomorrow. Ronny has got a lot of questions about the test. He must talk to his teacher. Ronny must not be late today.
This morning he is only in the bathroom for four minutes. Where is his school uniform? Oh good, it is on the chair. But where are his black shoes? He cannot find them. There they are, behind the door. It is a quarter past eight. The Bennetts' house is a long way from school, and Ronny has only got half an hour.

Ronny has a glass of milk and a banana for breakfast – no time for toast with butter and jam today.
It is ten to nine. Ronny is five minutes late. But his teacher is not in the classroom. Ronny's German teacher is ill today. Great! No German test tomorrow!

Verbesserungen:

So schreibe ich die Wörter richtig:

DIKTAT

16 A phone call

(Anne:) Hello, Steve. Where are your parents? Are they in their new shop?

(Steve:) No, they aren't, they're in the garden.

(Anne:) And Kevin? Is he in the garden, too?

(Steve:) No, he isn't. He's at the circus with his friend Dan.

(Anne:) And Kate? Is she at the circus, too?

(Steve:) No, she isn't. She's in her room. She can't go to the circus, she's ill. Kate's in bed with her teddy-bear and a comic.

Verbesserungen:

So schreibe ich die Wörter richtig:

DIKTAT

17 At the circus

This week, there is a circus in town. Tom, Betty and Molly Parker are there.
Look, the animals are coming – two big grey elephants and eight white horses.
Next comes a little brown bear, it is riding on a child's bike.
What's next? Three acrobats are coming in. One of them is flying through the air and the other two are catching him.
Now the children's best friend is coming – the clown. Just look at his funny clothes! He's wearing a yellow hat. His T-shirt is pink and blue, his trousers are too short, his left shoe is brown and his right shoe is red.
It really is a great show.
At home in the evening Tom and Molly are telling their parents about the circus. But where is Betty? Here she is. She has got Molly's little sunhat on her head and she is wearing a pair of big shoes of different colours – her daddy's left brown shoe and her mum's right red shoe. The Parkers are laughing, only Molly is crying. She wants her sunhat. She wants to be a clown, too.

Verbesserungen:

So schreibe ich die Wörter richtig:

DIKTAT

18 Kate takes photos

On Friday, Kate's class goes on a short trip to the countryside. When the coach comes, the pupils get on quickly because they all want to have a window seat.
Who's still missing? Kate is, as usual. She comes five minutes late.
The weather is wonderful. The coach stops near a river, and all the pupils get off and have a picnic. Later, they play ball, go for a walk, or watch the horses and the ponies in the fields.
Kate is always interested in horses. She climbs up a wall to take a photo of a beautiful white horse from the top of the wall. Her teacher tells her to be careful, but it is too late. Kate falls off the wall and drops the camera. Kate almost cries. It is not her camera. Whose camera is it? It's Kevin's. Kate is lucky, her brother's camera is all right, and she is all right, too.

Verbesserungen:

So schreibe ich die Wörter richtig:

DIKTAT

19 Holidays in Scotland

Every year our English friends go to Scotland for their summer holidays. They rent a holiday flat in a house two miles from the sea. They like the coast and they are outside in the sunshine and fresh air all day long.
In June and July it is often very sunny there. They have breakfast in the garden – toast and marmalade or jam with tea or coffee. They swim in the sea, but not too long, because the water is a bit cold. Sometimes they go fishing in a small boat.
They say that holidays in Scotland are not expensive. They do not go to restaurants. They buy fresh eggs, milk and vegetables from a farmer, and fresh fish from a fisherman, and they make their own dinner in the kitchen of their holiday flat.
On the beach there are other tourists, too. Americans, French and Germans. They all speak English, of course.
Our friends are always unhappy when the holidays are over. They say that we must come with them to Scotland next time. It is a wonderful country.

Verbesserungen:

So schreibe ich die Wörter richtig:

DIKTAT

20 Kate's letter to Ann

Dear Ann,

My holidays begin on Wednesday 12 July. No school, no homework, no books, no teachers for seven weeks! It's just great.
Can you come and stay with me for a week or so? Kevin is on the Parkers' farm with his German friend Kim. My parents are working at their newspaper shop, so I'm alone in the house all day long. Kevin is a terrible brother, but when he's not here, it's a bit boring.
When you come you can sleep in Kevin's room. There are a lot of interesting things to do here. On Friday, there's a big horse show in town. In the evening, there's a disco for young people at the youth club.
Saturday is Tom's birthday. I've got an invitation to his party and I'm sure you can come, too. On Sunday, we can go to Adventureland near York. My parents want to visit Aunt Mary in York, so they can leave us at Adventureland for the afternoon and pick us up in the evening after their visit.
Please come! I'm sure we can have a great time.

Love,

Kate

Verbesserungen:

So schreibe ich die Wörter richtig:

DIKTAT

21 A letter to a penfriend (*oder:* pen-friend)

Dear Lukas,

Today I want to tell you about Aunt Susan and Uncle John. They live in a house on the River Thames ten miles south of Oxford. They love the river. Our uncle is English, but Aunt Susan is a German. She speaks English very well. I only have one aunt and one uncle. Uncle John is my dad's brother. My brother and I visited them last Easter. Easter Sunday was a warm day but the water is too cold for swimming in spring, so we just walked along the river. We had a glass of Coke at a small café in the High Street. We had a wonderful time. We want to visit them in summer – in August perhaps. That's all for today,

Love,
Hilary

Verbesserungen:

So schreibe ich die Wörter richtig:

___

___

___

___

___

___

___

___

___

DIKTAT

22 A questionnaire for the school magazine

This is what Emma wrote on a questionnaire about her school:
Name: Emma Smith
Address: 10, High Street
Favourite subjects: My favourite subjects are English and French. I like music, too. I play the guitar in the school orchestra. I don't like history or sport much, except swimming.
Sports: From October to March I swim in the school team. We often win matches against other schools.
Clubs and activities: Activities should begin earlier – before half past four. We don't need school groups for tennis or squash. You can do these at any sports centre.
School cafeteria: We need more fresh vegetables and salads. And who wants hot tomato soup in summer? I would like a glass of fruit juice with my meals not just tea, hot chocolate or Coke!

Verbesserungen:

So schreibe ich die Wörter richtig:

DIKTAT

23 A boat trip to Lundy Island

If you really want to see the sea you won't want to miss a boat trip to Lundy Island. Our boats only take an hour to get to the island. Enough time to meet new friends. Then you can walk around the island and see the most interesting things. There is more to see than you think. You can see and hear the sea-birds here. This is somewhere where you can wear your oldest clothes! Bring your own food or buy a meal in one of the restaurants. Write postcards to your friends with Lundy Island stamps! Take a break from lying in the sun. Bring your sons and daughters, too. Two children go free with two parents.

Verbesserungen:

So schreibe ich die Wörter richtig:

____

____

____

____

____

____

____

____

____

____

DIKTAT

24 An autumn holiday in Scotland

Guess what we did in the autumn holidays? We visited friends in Scotland. It rained for two days and two nights, but after that the weather was fine. Our friends knew the right place for a picnic. They often went there. It was an old castle right next to a lake with an island in the middle. Our friends said we would be there in half an hour. But they were wrong. We needed three-quarters of an hour. We had a lot of things with us: sandwiches, biscuits, knives, plates, cups, bottles of water, so we couldn't walk fast. John even brought his guitar! He thought it was a good idea. We walked through the high grass and climbed the hill to the castle. After the picnic we talked and listened to John's guitar.

Verbesserungen:

So schreibe ich die Wörter richtig:

DIKTAT 25

Country cousins

My brother and I lived in the country when we were young. All our cousins lived in big towns. We sometimes visited them in the holidays. One summer we went to London to stay with our aunt. Aunt Kate had one son and two daughters. The boy's name was Kevin and the girls were called Melanie and Emma. Aunt Kate worked at a German restaurant near Victoria Station. Kevin was some years older than us, but the girls were younger, and we liked them more than their brother. Sometimes we heard Kevin use the words "country cousins" when he was talking about us to his city friends. But we weren't worried. We soon learned that Kevin hated living in London. He really wanted to live in the country, too.

Verbesserungen:

So schreibe ich die Wörter richtig:

DIKTAT

26 A Christmas letter

Dear Lisa,

Thank you for your letter and for the photo of the basketball team you're in. Who's the girl on your left in the photo? Is it your sister? Whose is the dog in front of the team? It's got its paws on the ball! How funny!
It's only five days until Christmas now. I've done my Christmas shopping, so I needn't go into town again. School's over for two weeks. I got my school report yesterday, but you won't want to hear about that!
What's New Year like in Northern Germany? You have fireworks, don't you? There aren't any fireworks at New Year in England.
I mustn't make this letter too long, and I can't think of any more news. Write soon.

Love,

Peter

Verbesserungen:

So schreibe ich die Wörter richtig:

DIKTAT

27 A good idea or not?

Two hundred years ago there were no rabbits in Australia. People brought them from Europe as pets or for food. Four years later there were already more rabbits than people. Forty years later there were rabbits over half the country. The rabbits ate almost all the grass. The poor sheep farmers! What could they do? They wanted to kill them all. The farmers bought dogs and the dogs caught a lot of the rabbits. Then the daughter of one of the sheep farmers got an idea. She was a doctor. She thought that she could bring a disease to Australia to kill the rabbits but not the sheep. She talked to her father about her idea but he only laughed. She tried her idea. It killed half of Australia's rabbits in four years.

Verbesserungen:

So schreibe ich die Wörter richtig:

DIKTAT

28 On a plane

Good afternoon, ladies and gentlemen. Welcome on board our seventy-six-seat plane. We are already fifteen minutes late today, but everybody is on board now and we can take off in a moment. Please sit down now. Everything is all ready for take-off. Our flight to Birmingham is only thirty-five minutes. Always remember: you may not smoke anywhere inside the plane. The air temperature outside the airport building at Birmingham is twenty-seven degrees and the weather is good so you won't need your warm pullovers! T-shirts will be warm enough. If this is your first flight, don't worry. It's my ninety-second flight this year. I fly to Birmingham and back every day. Is everybody happy now? Have a nice flight!

Verbesserungen:

So schreibe ich die Wörter richtig:

DIKTAT

29 Where are the car keys?

It is Saturday afternoon. The Bennetts are at home. The Bennetts' two taxis are in the garage. At three o'clock Mrs Bennett must drive Mrs Jones to the station. Mrs Jones lives at 5 York Road. It is a big new house over the bridge next to the new hotel. But Mrs Bennett can't find her car keys. They aren't on the desk and they aren't in her pocket. Ronny is in the office. He's playing a computer game on the office computer. He hasn't got the keys. Oh dear! Where can they be? It is nearly three o'clock now! A good taxi driver must not be late!

Timmy is in the garage. He's playing with his matchbox cars. He is a good taxi driver – the best taxi driver in town! And he's got Mrs Bennett's keys. It is five past three now. Mrs Bennett is late. She is a bad taxi driver!

Verbesserungen:

So schreibe ich die Wörter richtig:

DIKTAT

30 The sandwich

It is Saturday evening. The Johnsons are having their meal. The weather is fine. Tomorrow is Sunday, and they all want to go to the seaside. Kate thinks that this is the best idea of the week. The next morning Mr and Mrs Johnson make tea and sandwiches for a picnic. They make cheese and ham sandwiches. Kate does not like butter, cheese or ham. She makes herself some sandwiches with margarine and egg.

The Johnsons leave at about half past nine and they arrive at the seaside at eleven. There are already lots of people at the beach, they are lying in the sun or swimming in the sea. The children are building sand castles or playing ball. Soon, Kevin and Kate are hungry, so they fetch their sandwiches. Kate cannot find her sandwich. Kevin has got it. Butter or margarine tastes the same to him. Kate tries to take her sandwich from Kevin. Kevin drops it in the sand. There is some margarine, egg and a lot of sand on it. Kevin says she can have her sandwich, but Kate replies he can keep it. It is a real sand sandwich now.

Verbesserungen:

So schreibe ich die Wörter richtig:

DIKTAT

31 A holiday letter

Hi, John!

We arrived here on Saturday last week, and we will be here for another three days. The weather is good and the food is OK, too. Who do you think we met on the beach yesterday? My English teacher! She's here with her two children. She couldn't see me because I was swimming in the sea and the beach was very full. She was talking to two other women. I thought I saw your neighbours, the Smiths, but I couldn't be sure. Do they have a new, blue car? I hope I don't meet any more people from our town! Mum and Dad don't go swimming. They just take off their shoes and put their feet in the sea. Well, that's my news for today. See you soon!

Love,

Carol

Verbesserungen:

So schreibe ich die Wörter richtig:

____

____

____

____

____

____

____

____

____

LÖSUNGEN

Hinweis: Bei den Lösungen wurde nur eine mögliche Antwort angegeben. Sowohl die Langformen (she is, cannot, is not usw.) als auch die Kurzformen (she's, can't isn't usw.) sind als richtig zu betrachten.

1 Substantive

ÜBUNG **1**

a) There are Mr Mason and his wife on the farm. There are a cock and a few geese, some hens, a cat, a dog and some pigs on the farm, too.

b)

nouns in the singular	nouns in the plural
a farmhouse	farmhouses
a wife	wives
a dog	dogs
a pig	pigs
a cock	cocks
a hen	hens
a goose	geese
a chimney	chimneys
an apple-tree	apple-trees

ÜBUNG **2**

a dog, a pony, a cow, a duck, a goose, a bull, a mouse, a horse

ÜBUNG **3**

There are a lot of men, women and children – presents – two boys – hand – present – teddy – one foot – one arm – one eye – mice – cake

ÜBUNG **4**

are – them – they are – it is – are

ÜBUNG **5**

a) I'm wearing ... (I am wearing) b) I like ... best.

2 Das Personalpronomen

ÜBUNG 1

1. He is on the farm.
2. She is in the house.
3. He is at school.
4. It is at school, too.
5. He is on his potty.
6. They are on the floor.
7. They are on his bed.
8. She is not at home.
9. She is with her.
10. They are in the park.

ÜBUNG 2

	Mögliche Antworten:
Where are Tom and Mike?	They are at home/not here/ill ...
Where is your homework?	It's at home/on the desk/on the bus/in my schoolbag ...
Where is your English book?	It's in my schoolbag/on the desk/at home/not here.
Where is your book?	It's in my schoolbag/on the desk/at home/not here.
Where is Christine?	She's ill/not here/at home ...
Where is the register?	It's on the desk/in my schoolbag/not here.
Where are they from?	They are from York.
Where are you from?	I'm from York, too.
Where is Kate?	She is in the classroom/at home/not here ...

ÜBUNG 3

1. I can't find them.
2. I can't find it.
3. I can't see/hear you.
4. I can't see him.
5. I can't see them.
6. I can't find them.
7. I can't find them.
8. I can't see it.
9. I can't find him.
10. I can't see it.
11. I can't see/find it.
12. I can't see/find them.

ÜBUNG 4

Kate:	Timmy:
I can't see you.	I'm here.
	It's not here. I can't find it.
	It's in my bed. I can see it from here.
I can't see them.	–
Where are they?	They are in my room.
Why are you crying?	They are bad trousers.
Are they wet again?	Yes, they are.
Let's wash them. Help me.	

ÜBUNG 5

Kate: Where are they? Help me to look for them. Are they under your bed?
Timmy: No, they aren't. They aren't there.
Kate: Where are they then? Let me guess. Are they in your bed?
Timmy: No, they aren't in my bed. They are in my teddy's bed.
Kate: Where is it?
Timmy: It's here.
Kate: But why are they in your teddy's bed?
Timmy: It's my teddy who makes them wet, not me.
Kate: Then call your teddy and tell him to help me.

3 Der bestimmte und der unbestimmte Artikel

ÜBUNG 1

an English book
a German book
an empty bottle
a workbook
a pencil-case
a water-pistol
an exercise book
an apple
an old sandwich

ÜBUNG 2

1. He is a milkman.
2. He is a postman.
3. He is a butcher.
4. He is a greengrocer.
5. She is a shop assistant.
6. She is a reporter.
7. He is a fireman.
8. He is a vet.

ÜBUNG 3

a)
[ðɪ] the old women
[ðɪ] the English children
[ðɪ] the example
[ðə] the yellow apples
[ðə] the young girls
[ðə] the silly answer
[ðə] the bad ideas
[ðɪ] the afternoons
[ðɪ] the American cars
[ðə] the difficult questions
[ðə] the school uniforms
[ðɪ] the empty pages

ÜBUNG 4

1. Boys like girls.
2. Tom likes Jenny.
3. Do you like the boys in your class?
4. Do you usually like girls more than boys?
5. What about the girls in your class?
6. Which of the boys/girls do you like best?
7. Who is the nicest boy/girl in your class?
8. What's the name of the girl/boy you like best?

9. Are the boys/girls in your class good at English?
10. Are boys as clever as girls?

ÜBUNG 5

Jenny is not Tom's sister, she is Tom's friend – in Apple Street – Apple Street is – in the north of York – to school by bus – to school by bike – Tom is – all the girls and boys – she likes Tom – the nicest boy – like Tom – likes maths – Maths is the subject – before tests – helps Tom – likes pets

ÜBUNG 6

Jenny goes to the same school as Tom – takes them to school in the morning – The school they go to is a big school. – a lot of pupils – like school – she likes school – most of her teachers – she can't go to school – stay in bed – a temperature – a cold – a bad headache – a/the doctor – stay in bed

ÜBUNG 7

Mögliche Antworten:
I can go to Germany by plane/by train ...
I can go to Scotland by train/by car/by taxi/by bike/by motor-bike/on foot ...
I can go to Ireland by plane/by boat ...
I can go to Denmark by plane/by boat ...
I can go to France by plane/by train/by ferry...
I can go to the Isle of Wight by boat/by train ...
I can go to Wales by train/by plane/by bus/by car ...

4 Substantive und ihre Begleiter

ÜBUNG 1

1. It's their farm.
2. It's their flat.
3. It's their car.
4. It's his sister.
5. It's her brother.
6. They are his toys.
7. It's his camera.
8. It's her boyfriend.

ÜBUNG 2

1. It's not your exercise book, it's Kate's. It's her exercise book.
2. ... when you keep it under your bed? What will her teacher say?
3. I think they are his keys.
4. This is not your picture book, it's Kate's. It was her birthday present ...
5. ... here's your teddy, ... your van, ... your telephone. So play with your things now.

ÜBUNG 3

1. What about your room? Do you like it?
2. Do you clean it or does your mother clean it?
3. What's in your room?
4. Is there anything under your bed?
5. Where do you keep your clothes?
6. Where do you do your homework?
7. Have you got a TV in your room?
8. Have you got posters and photos in your room, too?

ÜBUNG 4

There are a lot of things – There are books – They are on the chairs – And there is something – It's an old pullover – There are some socks – There are holes in them and they look dirty – There are a lot of photos – that photo over there – It's a photo – It's not a new bike, but its handlebars and its saddle are new.

ÜBUNG 5

Timmy:	Tom:
1. Is this your classroom?	1. This isn't my classroom.
2. Is this your class?	2. Yes, this is my class.
3. And that class over there?	3. That's Kate's class.
4. Is this your chair here?	4. ... that chair over there, that's Jenny's.
5. What's the name of that fat boy?	
6. Is that a teacher over there?	
7. But that's a teacher,Tom.	7. Ah yes, that's our English teacher.

ÜBUNG 6

No, Timmy, this isn't your biro/pen/rubber/ruler. It's Kate's. Look! Your biro/pen/rubber/ruler is over there.

No, Timmy, these aren't your socks/cassettes/keys/pencils/shoes. They are Kate's. Look! Your socks/cassettes/keys/pencils/shoes are over there.

ÜBUNG 7

1. How much homework ...
2. How much time ...
3. How many minutes ...
4. How many hours ...
5. How many subjects ...
6. How much help ...
7. How many tests ...
8. How many good marks ...
9. How many tests ...
10. How much money ...

ÜBUNG 8

... too many tests.
... too many bad marks.
... too many teachers.
... too much homework.
... too much work.
... too many questions.
... too many boring subjects.
... too much time indoors.
... so much.

5 Der s- und of-Genitiv

ÜBUNG 1

Timmy's toys
our cat's food
the man's boots
Jenny's dog
the boys' teacher
Kate's friends
the children's books
the Masons' house
the girls' schoolbags
women's clothes
the girls' school uniforms
my parents' car

ÜBUNG 2

	Mögliche Antworten:
Are these your toys, Tom?	No, they aren't. They are my baby brother's.
Is this your girlfriend, Kevin?	No, it isn't. It's Tom's.
Is this your magazine, Jenny?	No, it isn't. It's the girls'.
Is this your cat, Kate?	No, it isn't. It's my mother's.
Is this your homework, Joe?	No, it isn't. It's Kevin's.
Is this your house, Mr Mason?	No, it isn't. It's my grandparents'.
Is this your bike, Kate?	No, it isn't. It's Jenny's.
Is this your room, Tom?	No, it isn't. It's my sister's.
Is this your teddy, Jenny?	No, it isn't. It's Timmy's.
Is this your van, Timmy?	Yes, it is.

ÜBUNG 3

... Tom's baby brother – one of his favourite toys – he's got (he has got) other toys, too – other things – there's (there is) one of Jenny's letters – there's (there is) an old German book and there's (there is) Kate's ruler – some keys – his parents' keys – there's (there is) a tennis ball – Is it Kevin's or Joe's – It can't be Kate's or Tom's ...

ÜBUNG 4

Genitiv
... Tom's girlfriend
Jenny's other relatives
Jenny's first visit.

Kurzform
She's twelve (she is)
she's only got (she has only got) her parents.
it's (it is) her grandparents' house
she's got (she has got) an aunt
... who's (who is) over sixty and who's got (who has got) a flat

ÜBUNG 5

the boys' legs
the doors of my room
Kate's books
on the evening of my birthday
the girl's hands
the dog's feet
the children's clothes
the light of the moon
the windows of the car
my neighbour's cat
the end of school
Jenny's story

ÜBUNG 6

Mögliche Lösungen:
a bar of chocolate
lots of chocolate/food...
a glass of milk/tea
a cup of milk/tea
a plate of strawberries...
a tin of peas
a pound of cheese/sausages
a bag of crisps
a packet of cornflakes
a piece of cheese

ÜBUNG 7

five bags of crisps
three packets of biscuits
five bottles of coke
five bottles of lemonade
three pounds of sausages
two tins of pineapples
five packets of ice cream

ÜBUNG 8

"Get off that bike – on Tom's bike – they will fall off the bike – So Mike took one hand out of his pocket – not very far from the corner shop to the Masons' flat – the bottles fell off the bike – two bottles of lemonade – to Mrs White's shop – no bottles fell off the bike – both hands out of his pockets – into Tom's room – a telephone call from Jenny's mother – she has just come home from school – greetings from Jenny and from my husband – you will hear from Jenny tomorrow.

6 Das Präsens von „haben"

ÜBUNG **1**

1. They have got a flat.
2. They have got five rooms.
3. Tom has got a room, and Kate has got a room, too.
4. Timmy hasn't got a big room.
5. The Masons have got a car.
6. Tom and Kate haven't got a car, they have got bikes.
7. Timmy hasn't got a bike ...
8. But he has got two big toy cars ...

ÜBUNG **2**

a) I have got a cat, a dog, a teddy, two buckets, a telephone, some toy cars, some picture books etc.

b) I have got ...

ÜBUNG **3**

a) Kate hasn't got a sister/a boyfriend/a car/a teddy/a dog/TV/but she has got two brothers, a lot of friends/a bike/toy cars/a football/a radio.

b) I have got ... , but I haven't got ...

c) My friend has got .../They have got ...

ÜBUNG **4**

a) Has Kate got two brothers/a lot of friends/a bike/toy cars/a football/a radio? Yes, she has.
Has she got a sister/a boyfriend/a car/a teddy/a dog/TV? No, she hasn't.

b) Have you got a brother/a lot of friends/a bike/a teddy/a football/a radio...?Yes, I have./No, I haven't.

ÜBUNG **5**

Beispiele für Lösungen:
Have you got a car? No, I haven't.
Has your mother got a water-pistol? No, she hasn't.
Has your English teacher got a toy car? No, he hasn't.
Have your friends got a lot of toys? Yes, they have.

7 Das Präsens von „sein"

ÜBUNG 1

... it is Tom's birthday – He is twelve – all his friends are there – his sister is there – Her name is Kate – She is eleven years old – Only Jenny is not there – Where is she? – She is ill – They are all – it is full of children – They are all hungry – There are a lot of sandwiches – there are some bottles – But one bottle is on the floor – it is broken and there is a pool – And who is in the pool? – It is Timmy ...

ÜBUNG 2

That is Kevin and that is Joe.
They are my best friends.
They are in my class.

And that boy over there is Bill.
He is in my class, too, and he is very good at maths. In tests he can be very useful.

That is my sister! Her name is Kate. All her teachers are very happy when she is ill. And I am happy when she is back at school again!

And this is my baby brother.
His name is Timmy. He is three years old.

ÜBUNG 3

1. No, it isn't.
2. No, she isn't.
3. No, he isn't.
4. No, she isn't.
5. Yes, she is.
6. Yes, it is.
7. Yes, there are.
8. No, they aren't.
9. Yes, they are.
10. Yes, it is.

Weitere Möglichkeiten:

Are all his friends there?	Yes, they are.
Is Kate there, too?	Yes, she is.
Is she ten years old?	No, she isn't.
etc.	

ÜBUNG 4

Is it a thing? No, it isn't.
Is it an animal? No, it isn't.
Is it in this room? No, it isn't.
Is it a toy? No, it isn't.
Is it something nice? No, it isn't.
Is it something terrible? Yes, it is.
It is a woman? No, it isn't.
Is it a man? Yes, it is.
Is he old? Yes, he is.
Is he at our school? Yes, he is.
Is it a teacher? Yes, it is.
Is it our maths teacher? Yes, it is.

ÜBUNG 5

Who is Jenny?
How old is she?
Is she a nice girl?
Why isn't she here?
Where is she now?
Are her parents at home?
What has she got?
Has she got a temperature?
Has she got brothers and sisters?
Is she from York?

ÜBUNG 6

1. Is Jenny eleven?
2. Is she a nice girl?
3. Is she your girlfriend?
4. Why isn't she here/at your party?
5. What has she got?
6. Has she got a temperature?
7. Where is she?

8 Die Verlaufsform des Präsens

ÜBUNG 1

coming, lying, drying, calling, cutting, dancing, drinking, flying, listening, making, getting, playing, putting, running, sitting, swimming, tying, watching

ÜBUNG 2

1. Mike is taking photos.
2. John is sitting at the table and drinking all the lemonade.
3. Kate is skipping.
4. Tom is ringing up Jenny.
5. Betty is flirting with Kevin.
6. Some boys are playing football.
7. Some girls are dancing in the kitchen.
8. Ann is lying on the floor and watching a film on TV.
9. Jim and Barbara are eating sandwiches.
10. Susan is sitting in a corner and reading a magazine.

ÜBUNG 3

1. That's not right, Timmy. Mike isn't playing with his camera, he's taking photos.
2. John isn't eating all the sandwiches, he's drinking all the lemonade.
3. Kate isn't hopping around like a rabbit, she's skipping.
4. Tom isn't talking to his teacher, he's ringing up Jenny.
5. Betty isn't talking nonsense to Kevin, she's flirting with him.
6. The boys aren't quarrelling about a ball; they are playing football.
7. The girls aren't running around in the kitchen, they are dancing.
8. Ann isn't lying on the floor because she is ill. She's lying on the floor because she is watching a film on TV.
9. Jim and Barbara aren't making sandwiches, they are eating them.
10. Susan isn't reading your picture book, she's reading a magazine.

ÜBUNG 4

1. Is Mike really playing with his camera?	Yes, he is.
2. Is John really eating all the sandwiches?	Yes, he is.
3. Is Kate really hopping around like a rabbit?	Yes, she is.
4. Is Tom really talking to his teacher?	Yes, he is.
5. Is Betty really talking nonsense to Kevin?	Yes, she is.
6. Are some boys really quarrelling about a ball?	Yes, they are.
7. Are some girls really running around in the kitchen?	Yes, they are.
8. Is Ann really lying on the floor because she is ill?	Yes, she is.
9. Are Jim and Barbara really making sandwiches?	Yes, they are.
10. Is Susan really reading your picture book?	Yes, she is.

ÜBUNG 5

– What are you doing, Kate?	I'm skipping.
– Are you talking to your teacher, Tom?	No, I'm talking to Jenny.
– What are you doing with your camera, Mike?	I'm taking photos.
– Are you reading my picture book, Susan?	No, I'm reading a magazine.
– Why are you lying on the floor, Ann?	I'm watching a film.
– What are you doing with the ball?	We are playing football.
– What are you doing in the kitchen?	We are dancing.
– What are you doing, John?	I'm drinking lemonade.
– What are you doing, Jim and Barbera?	We're eating sandwiches.

ÜBUNG 6

First scene:
When is the party over?
Where are the children going?
What are they?
Who is happy, too?
Where is he?
Where is he lying?
What isn't he doing?
Who is playing with Tom's birthday presents?
Where are they now?

Second scene:
Where is Timmy still lying?
What has he got in his hand?
What is he drawing?

Third scene:
Who is coming upstairs?
What is he shouting?
What is he doing?
What is he opening?

9 Modale Hilfsverben

ÜBUNG 1

1. He needn't go to school.
2. He can go to kindergarten.
3. He can play with other children there.
4. Must he go there every day?
5. No, he needn't.

6. Can/may he go there alone?
7. No, he can't/may not/mustn't.
8. Can/may he take his bike?
9. No, he can't/may not/mustn't.
10. Must Tom fetch him in the afternoon?
11. Yes, he must fetch him on Thursdays and Fridays.

ÜBUNG **2**

1. No, that's wrong. Kate can go to her room.
2. No, that's wrong. She must help her mother.
3. No, that's wrong. Tom must help his mother to wash up the dishes and to clean the kitchen floor, but he needn't clean Kate's room.
4. No, that's wrong. He must help to wash them up.
5. That's right.
6. That's wrong. He needn't clean them.
7. That's right. Timmy can help him with the dishes.
8. That's wrong. He needn't clean it.
9. That's wrong. He mustn't drop them.
10. That's right. He can stay up a little longer.

ÜBUNG **3**

Tom	Jenny's mother
1. Can/may I talk to Jenny, please?	Sorry, Tom, you can't/may not.
2. Can Jenny come tomorrow?	No, she can't. She can't/may not/mustn't get up.
3. Must she stay in bed all day?	Yes, she must.
4. Must she take medicine?	No, she needn't.
5. Can/may I see her this afternoon?	No, you can't/may not see her today. She must go to the doctor's.

ÜBUNG **4**

1. I mustn't go to school.
2. I must stay in bed.
3. I mustn't watch too much TV.
4. I must take my temperature every day.
5. I must take my medicine.
6. I must come to his surgery again on Monday at 4 o'clock.
7. I mustn't play with my friends.

ÜBUNG 5

She must take her medicine.
She mustn't ride on her bike.
She mustn't go to school.
She needn't do her homework.
She can ring up her friends.
She can write letters.
She can watch TV.
She can read a book.
She needn't/mustn't clean her room.
She needn't/mustn't help her mother.
She can listen to music.
She mustn't play football.

ÜBUNG 6

1. A good patient must do what the doctor tells him/her.
2. A good patient must tell the doctor what he/she has got.
3. A good patient must take medicine.
4. A good patient must stay in bed when he/she is ill.
5. A good patient needn't clean the doctor's car.
6. A good patient mustn't forget his/her appointment.
7. Correct
8. A good patient must listen to his/her doctor.
9. A good patient needn't clean the doctor's surgery.

ÜBUNG 7

1. No, you needn't.
2. No, you needn't.
3. Yes, you must.
4. No, you can't.
5. Yes, you can.
6. Yes, you must.
7. Yes, they may, ...
8. Yes, you may.
9. Yes, you must.

ÜBUNG 8

– Are you very ill?	Yes, I am.
– Must you stay in bed?	Yes, I must.
– Must you stay indoors all day?	Yes, I must.
– May you get up for an hour or two?	Yes, I may.
– Have you got a temperature?	Yes, I have.
– Can you go to school on Thursday?	No, I can't.
– Are you happy that you needn't go to school?	Yes, I am.
– Are your teachers happy, too?	No, they aren't.

ÜBUNG 9

Shall I do the shopping for you?
Shall I clean the rooms?
Shall I go to the chemist's?
Shall I get your medicine?
Shall I open the window?
Shall I look after my brother/sister?
Shall I cook the meals?
Shall I do the washing-up?
Shall I make your bed?
Shall I make you some tea?
Shall I ring up the doctor?

10 Das Präsens von Vollverben

ÜBUNG 1

1. He gets up ...
2. Then he washes and puts on his clothes.
3. Then he goes down ...
4. There he has breakfast.
5. Then he looks for his schoolbag.
6. After that he leaves the house.
7. Then he goes to the bus stop.
8. He usually takes the bus ...
9. He arrives ...

ÜBUNG 2

a)
1. Mike and Tom play football ...
2. Sam eats his sandwiches.
3. Sandra does her English homework.
4. Anne talks to Betty.
5. John copies his homework ...
6. Kevin runs around ...
7. Bob and David make a lot of noise ...
8. Pam cleans the board.
9. Jane and Sharon write letters.

b) Mögliche Antworten:
1. I do my homework.
2. I learn English.
3. I talk to my neighbour.
4. I clean the board.
5. I sing a song.

ÜBUNG 3

1. They don't get up in the morning.
2. They don't have an early breakfast.
3. Mr Brown doesn't wash his car.
4. Mrs Brown doesn't do the cooking.
5. Often, their children don't go to school.
6. They don't like school.
7. Helen doesn't like her teachers.
8. She doesn't do her homework.

ÜBUNG 4

Tom likes bananas, but he doesn't like oranges.
He likes Jenny, but he doesn't like Ben.
Jenny and Kate like volleyball, but they don't like tennis.
They like sports, but they don't like all sports.
Timmy likes cornflakes, but he doesn't like tea.
He likes dogs, but he doesn't like cats.
Mike likes photos, but he doesn't like comics.
He likes music, but he doesn't like singing.
The Browns don't like work, but they like sleeping.
They don't like books, but they like TV.

ÜBUNG 5

Mögliche Lösungen:
I like tennis, but my mother doesn't.
I don't like maths, but my neighbour does.
My friends like pop music, but my parents don't.
My parents don't like Kate, but I do.
etc.

ÜBUNG 6

– Do you like it here?
– Does your mother like York?
– Do you like English?
– Do you like school?
– Do you play hockey?
– Do you go to school by bike?
– Do you like sports?
– Does your sister go to our school, too?
– Do you play an instrument?
– Does your father work in York?

ÜBUNG 7

1. Do you like your class?
2. Do you like all the subjects?
3. Do you like maths?
4. Do you like all the teachers?
5. Do you often forget your homework?
6. Do you come to school by bus?
7. Do you come to school by bike in winter, too?
8. Do you play football?
9. Do your parents live in York, too?
10. Do you do your homework in the afternoon?

ÜBUNG 8

1.	Where do you live?	I live in ...
2.	When do you get up in the morning?	I get up at ...
3.	When does your mother get up?	She gets up at ...
4.	What do you have for breakfast?	I have ... for breakfast.
5.	Why don't you like cornflakes?	I don't like them because ...
6.	When do your parents leave the house?	They leave the house at ...
7.	When do they come home again?	They come home again at ...
8.	How do you get to school?	I get to school by ...
9.	Why don't you take the bus?	I don't take it because ...
10.	What do you do in the afternoon?	In the afternoon, I ...
11.	What games do you like?	I like ...
12.	What do you do in the evening?	In the evening, I ...
13.	When do you go to bed?	I go to bed at ...
14.	When do you switch off the light?	I switch off the light at ...
15.	When do your parents go to bed?	They go to bed at ...

ÜBUNG 9

a)
1. When do you get up?
2. When do you start work?
3. When do you leave the house?
4. What do you drive?
5. Who do you collect from the villages?
6. Where do you take them?
7. When does school start?
8. When do you fetch them?
9. Where do you take them?
10. What do you clean then?
11. What do you often find in the bus?

b) I get up at 5.30, because work starts at seven o'clock. I leave my house at 6.30. I drive a school bus. I collect the children from the villages and take them to school. School starts at a quarter to nine. In the afternoon I fetch them from school and take them home again. Then I clean the bus. I often find things in the bus.

11 Die einfache Gegenwart und die Verlaufsform im Vergleich

ÜBUNG 1

1. Mike usually gets up at 7, but today he is still in bed. He is sleeping.
2. He usually has breakfast at 7.30, but today he is still lying in bed.
3. He often has little time to spend in the bathroom, but this morning he is taking a bath.
4. He usually puts on his school uniform, but today he is wearing his other clothes.
5. He usually has lunch at school, but today he is having lunch at home.
6. Mike usually helps his mother with the dishes. His father is washing the dishes.
7. His parents usually work in the afternoon, ... They are going for a walk.
   Do you know why? Well, it's Sunday.

ÜBUNG 2

Mögliche Antworten:
On Sundays I usually get up late/go for a walk/do my homework.
On Sundays I often watch TV/ring up my friends/play football/write letters.
On Sundays I sometimes cook lunch/help Mum and Dad/brush my shoes.
On Sundays I never clean my room/clean my bike/go to school/learn English.

ÜBUNG 3

1. Mike is taking a picture of his new school. He likes taking pictures.
2. He doesn't only take pictures of schools, he takes pictures of everything. Here he is taking a picture of Tom and Jenny.
3. He always puts his pictures in an album. Look! He is putting a picture in his album now.
4. He has already got a lot of albums. He keeps them in his room.

ÜBUNG 4

This is Dad. He is sitting in his bus.

This is Dad again. He is cleaning the bus.

This is our house. We live there now.

This is Mum. She is leaving the house. She always leaves at 8.

This is our garden. Look! Mum is working in it. She likes her garden.

This is our corner shop. Mum works there. She sells groceries.

ÜBUNG 5

First they break the eggs and put them in a bowl.
Then they add some milk, salt and pepper.
Then they stir the eggs.
Next they look for a frying pan.
Then they put fat in it.
Then they put the pan on the oven.
After that they put everything in the frying pan and stir two or three times.
Then they put the scrambled eggs on a plate.
Then they take the eggs upstairs and eat them.

ÜBUNG 6

a)
1. When do you usually get up?
2. When do you usually wash?
3. When do you usually have breakfast?
4. When do you usually get in your car?
5. When do you usually open the surgery?
6. When do you usually examine sick animals?
7. When do you usually have lunch/Where do you usually have lunch?
8. When do you usually leave the restaurant?
9. When do you usually have a cup of tea?
10. When do you usually close the door of the surgery?
11. When do you usually get home?

b) Mr Mason usually gets up at seven o'clock every morning. Then he washes and has breakfast. After that he gets in his car. He opens his surgery at 8.30. He examines sick animals between 9 and 12. Then he has lunch at a restaurant. He usually leaves the restaurant at 13.45. At 5 he usually has a cup of tea. He closes the door of his surgery at 5.30. He usually gets home at 6.

ÜBUNG 7

Mögliche Antworten:
I get up at ..., then I wash and have breakfast. Then I go to school. I usually get home at ... In the afternoon I first ..., then I ... After that I ... In the evenings I usually ... I go to bed at ...

ÜBUNG 8

... the sun is shining – the Masons are still sitting at the breakfast table – nobody is doing any work – Mr Mason isn't looking after animals – Mrs Mason – she works in a hospital as a nurse – isn't looking after her patients.
... The Masons always have a late breakfast – she is sleeping – Mr Mason asks – "What is she doing in her room?" – So Timmy goes to Kate's room – he opens the door and sees – he tries to wake her up, but Kate doesn't listen, so Timmy goes back and tells his dad that Kate is still sleeping – Mr Mason says – if she doesn't want to get up – Timmy fetches Tom's water-pistol and goes to Kate's room – somebody is shouting in an angry voice ...

12 Fragen, Kurzantworten und die Verneinung im Überblick

ÜBUNG 1

Dear Jenny,
I hope we can see each other this afternoon. I have got a lot of homework to do, but I think I can come ... I hope I can come. I really want to see you again. You are the nicest girl I know. I am always thinking of you. You know I like you.

ÜBUNG 2

Mögliche Antworten:
Jenny doesn't begin to cry.
She must laugh.
She writes a letter, too, and shows it to her neighbours.
They all begin to laugh.
She isn't very angry.
She doesn't go home immediately.

ÜBUNG 3

Jenny isn't ten years old, she is twelve.
Her parents have got a flat. They haven't got a house.
Her father has got a van. He hasn't got a car.

She doesn't go to school by bus. She goes to school by bike.
She likes maths, but she doesn't like English.
She has got a good maths teacher, but her English teacher is awful.
She doesn't like all the boys in her class, but she likes Tom.
She is sometimes late, but she isn't late very often.
She likes music, but she doesn't like singing.
She can play a lot of games, but she can't play football.
She is good at volleyball, but she is bad at swimming.

ÜBUNG 4

Mögliche Antworten:

I'm ..., I'm not ...	She is ..., she isn't ...
I've got ..., but I haven't got ...	She has got ..., but she hasn't got ...
My parents have got ..., but we haven't got ...	Her parents ...
We have got ..., but we haven't got ...	They have got ..., but they haven't got ...
I go to school by ...	She goes to ...
I like ..., but I don't like ...	She likes ..., but she doesn't like ...
I have got ..., but I haven't got ...	She has got ..., but she hasn't got ...
I don't like ..., but I like ...	She doesn't like ..., but she likes ...
I am often/never ..., but sometimes I ...	She is often/never ..., but sometimes I ...
I like ..., but I don't like ...	She likes ..., but she doesn't like ...
I can play ..., but I can't ...	She can play ..., but she can't play ...
I am good at ..., but I am bad at ...	She is good at ..., but she is bad at ...

ÜBUNG 5

Mögliche Antworten:
– That's wrong. Some of them do, but others don't.
– That's wrong. Good pupils aren't silly.
– That's wrong. Sometimes they forget things, too.
– That's wrong. Some of them have a lot of friends, others don't.
– That's wrong. Some of them make their teachers angry, too.
– That's wrong again. Good pupils talk in lessons, too.
– That's wrong. Good pupils aren't unhappy, but sometimes bad pupils are.
– That's wrong again. Some of them are bad at sports, but not all of them.
– That's wrong, too. Some of them do, but not all of them work too much.
– This is right. Good pupils usually do their homework.

ÜBUNG 6

- Are you often alone?
- Do you like your parents?
- Have you got any friends?
- Do you watch a lot of TV?
- Are most of your teachers nice?
- Are you often afraid?
- Have you got any hobbies?
- Do your parents often play with you?
- Have you got anybody to talk to?
- Do you often cry?
- Can you do what you want?
- Are your parents often out in the evening?

ÜBUNG 7

- Do you like school?
- Do you often forget your homework?
- Are you doing your homework now?
- Is your mum helping you now?
- Do your parents often help you?
- Have you got nice teachers?
- Do they like you?
- Do they give you a lot of homework?
- Can you talk during lessons?
- May you eat chewing gum in the English lessons?
- Have you got a school magazine at your school?
- Do you read it?
- Do you find it interesting?

ÜBUNG 8

- Do you find everything boring?
- Do you often sleep during lessons?
- Are you often late?
- Can you sit still?
- Do you talk all the time?
- Can you listen?
- Are you often ill for tests?
- Do you only like sports?
- Do you listen only when your teacher gets angry?
- Do you often forget things?
- Do you do your homework?

ÜBUNG 9

1. No, it isn't.
2. No, it isn't.
3. No, he isn't.
4. No, they aren't.
5. Yes, they are.
6. Yes, he is.
7. Yes, he does.
8. Yes, they are.
9. Yes, he is.
10. Yes, they do.
11. Yes, they do.
12. No, it isn't. It's a motor-bike.

ÜBUNG 10

1. Who is Tom's girlfriend?
2. Who is from Leeds?
3. What have they got?
4. Who is sometimes strict?
5. Who can't she always see?
6. What must she tell her parents?
7. Who must be back early?
   When must she be back?
8. When mustn't she be out?
9. What is ringing?
10. Where is Tom?

ÜBUNG 11

1. What have you got?
2. What is it?
3. What do you like/What do you do?
4. What must you buy for it?
5. Where must I go?
6. What must I lend you?
7. What do you want to buy?
9. What is very bad?
10. Who can't you understand?

ÜBUNG 12

1. How old is he?
2. Where does he sleep?
3. When do you usually get up?
4. What do you do then?
5. What does he usually have for breakfast?
6. When do you take him for a walk?
7. When do you go to work?
8. Where do you take him then?
9. How long does he stay there?
10. Where do you play?
11. What do you try to teach him?
12. What do you do in the evening?
13. What films does he like?
14. Why does he like westerns?

ÜBUNG 13

1. When can I see you again?
2. Where can we meet again?
3. How long can you stay?
4. When must you be back?
5. Why must you be back so early?
6. When must you help your mother?
7. What must you do?

13 Das will- und going to-Futur

ÜBUNG 1

I think the weather will be nice.
I hope we'll spend a nice day together.
I don't think it will rain.
Perhaps the sun will shine.
I hope the water won't be too cold.
If the water isn't too cold, we'll go for a swim.
We will spend the afternoon there.
I hope you'll have a good time.

ÜBUNG 2

Jenny:
When will we be there?
Will we need a warm pullover?
Will you buy us an ice cream?
Kevin:
Will we have lunch on the beach?
Will we play games on the beach?
Peter:
What games will we play?
Will we be allowed to walk around on our own?
Susan:
Will we have time enough to go shopping?
When will we be back?
Will the maths teacher come with us?

ÜBUNG 3

a) She hopes that the weather will be nice.
Perhaps it won't rain.
She is sure that they will have lots of fun.
She hopes that her friends will go, too.
She is sure that there will be a lot of interesting things to see.
She thinks that her pocket money will be enough.
She hopes that there won't be too many teachers.
She hopes that there won't be any homework for the next day.

b) Mögliche Antworten:
I hope the bus won't have a breakdown.
I hope our teachers will leave us alone.
I hope we won't have to visit that terrible museum.
Perhaps I'll find a nice present for my friend.
etc.

ÜBUNG 4

Mögliche Antworten:
If the coach is late, they won't leave at 8'clock.
If the coach breaks down, the driver won't be happy.
If it rains all day, they won't go to the beach.
If the sun doesn't shine, they won't go for a swim.
If some of the children are late, their teacher will be angry.
If Mr Benson is ill, there will be no excursion.
If Kate loses her pocket money, she will be unhappy.
If they take the wrong road, they will be late.

ÜBUNG 5

Mögliche Lösungen:
When they are on the beach, they will take off their clothes/they will play games/they will go for a swim/they will splash Mr Benson with water/they will have a picnic on the beach/they will be very noisy/they will run around/they will rush into the water/play softball/look for shells.

ÜBUNG 6

Catherine: I'll buy something to drink, too.
Jim: No problem. I'll help you.
Helen: I'll buy some, too.
Ronny: Well, then, I'll have a sandwich, too.

ÜBUNG 7

a) 1. ... she is going to work harder.
2. ... so she is going to help her.
3. ... so she isn't going to invite him.
4. ... She is going to write him this afternoon.
5. ... Her parents are going to buy her a new bike.
6. ... What is she going to do? Well, she is going to clean it.
7. ... She is going to go to the seaside.
8. ... She is going to spend her holiday there.

b) 1. What are you going to do about your tests, Kate? Are you going to work harder?
2. What are you going to do, Jenny? Are you going to help Kate?
3. What are you going to do, Kate? Are you going to invite Ronny?
4. What are you going to do this afternoon, Helen? Are you going to spend it with Ben?
5. What are your parents going to do, Linda? Are they going to buy you a new bike?
6. What are you going to do with your room, Betty? Are you going to clean it?
7. What are you going to do in your holidays, Mary? Are you going to go to the seaside?
8. What are you going to do there? Are you going to spend your holiday there?

ÜBUNG 8

1. If the weather is fine, we'll play in the garden.
2. I think everybody will like that.
3. But I hope Ronny won't come. I'm not going to invite him.
4. Perhaps Jenny will help me.
5. I hope Tom will help me with the lemonade. I will ask him when I see him.
6. Who is going to buy/will buy all the rest?
7. Well, I'll ask Mum if she ... Perhaps he will be tired tired when he gets back.

ÜBUNG 9

I'm going to ring up my friends.
I'm going to invite them.
I'll ask them if they can come.
I'm going to go to a supermarket to buy things.
I'll ask Dad if he can help me.
Perhaps he'll have time to help me.
I hope Mum will help me, too.
She will make chips and sausages for us if I ask her.
I hope she will let us use the dining-room if it rains.

ÜBUNG 10

1. Tomorrow we will (are going to) write an English test.
2. I hope it won't be too difficult.
3. I hope my neighbour will help me.
4. Perhaps I'll get a good mark then.
5. I'm going to ask her tonight if she wants to help me.
6. If she helps me, I'll give her a bar of chocolate.
7. But I'll only give it to her if I my mark is good.
8. If my mark is bad, I'll eat the bar of chocolate myself.

14 Das present perfect

ÜBUNG 1

a) lived, given; carried, played; said, lain; showed, felt; caught, thought; brought, told; left, bet; spent, stood; written, taken

b) to pay, to teach; to choose, to fall; to lose, to drop; to throw, to try; to feed, to buy

ÜBUNG 2

– They have booked a place for July.
– They have written to the local tourist office.
– They have bought a new road map.
– They have had a look at it.
– They have tried to find out the best route.
– They have begun to check their caravan.
– They have bought a new bottle of gas.
– They have cleaned the water tank.
– They have checked the tyres.
– They have repaired the rear window.

ÜBUNG **3**

We have washed the caravan, but we haven't cleaned the floor yet.
We have cleaned the windows, but we haven't made the beds yet.
We have put in some food, but we haven't bought a new frying pan yet.
We have taken Pete's tennis racket, but we haven't bought new tennis balls yet.
We have told the neighbours to look after the flowers, but we haven't given them a key yet.
We have put in Timmy's toys, but we haven't bought a new picture book yet.

ÜBUNG **4**

Have you put my telephone in the caravan?
Have you taken away my pencils?
Have you bought a new picture book for me?
Have you put it in the caravan?
Have you bought some chocolate?
Have you packed my swimming things?
Have you seen my teddy?
Have you found my red toy car?

ÜBUNG **5**

Mrs Mason:	Yes, we have.
Tom:	Yes, I have.
Kate:	Yes, I have.
All:	Yes, we have.
Tom:	Yes, I have.
Tom:	Yes, he has.
Timmy:	No, I haven't.
All:	No, we haven't.
Timmy:	No, we can't.

ÜBUNG **6**

Mögliche Fragen:

Have you ever been to a caravan site?	No, I haven't. I have never been to a caravan site.
Have you ever cleaned a caravan?	No, I haven't. I haven't cleaned a caravan yet.
Has your father ever had an accident?	No, he hasn't. He hasn't had an accident yet.
Has your sister ever been to England?	No, she hasn't. She hasn't been to England yet.
Have your friends ever slept in a caravan?	No, they haven't. They have never slept there.

etc.

ÜBUNG 7

1. The Masons have already packed everything.
2. They have put all their things in the caravan.
3. They have already done 100 kilometres.
4. But they have not arrived at their camping site yet.
5. Timmy has not been sick yet.
6. He has not had breakfast yet.
7. But he has already been on his potty four times.

ÜBUNG 8

1. I know what you told me.
2. Here it is.
3. He is angry now.
4. I know it.
5. I don't know it.
6. It is/looks dirty.

ÜBUNG 9

Jenny has kissed him goodbye.

He has found them again.

He has put it in the fridge.

They have packed everything.

Somebody has forgotten to shut it.

The Masons have left.

15 Das simple past

ÜBUNG 1

Regular verbs: stop, play, cry, carry

Irregular verbs: lead, read, sit, write, tear, catch, set, ride, hear, think, swim, feed, bring, teach, let, meet, lose, get, hit, hide, fly, break, say

ÜBUNG 2

The Masons wanted to leave – it was quite late when they got off – Kate was still tired – Tom wanted to finish a letter – Timmy's potty was missing – nobody knew where it was – When they were all in the car again, somebody saw that a window was still open – Mr Mason got out of the car, went into the house again and shut it – When he came back, Timmy wanted to go – So Mr Mason got out of the car – and carried Timmy to the bathroom – When they were back, they heard the telephone – So Tom got out of the car and ran into the house – he was not fast enough – When he arrived, the line was dead – finally they were ready to leave

ÜBUNG 3

They finally left at 11 o'clock. Their first stop was at 11.30 because Timmy was sick. They stopped again at 12.15 because Timmy was sick again. At 1 o'clock they had lunch, but when they left, they forgot Timmy's teddy. At 2 o'clock they got in their car again and drove on. As Mr Mason took a short cut, they lost two hours. They arrived at 6 o'clock at the camping site. There they tried to put up a tent for Tom, but it collapsed. They had supper at 8. At 9 they all went to bed because they were very tired.

ÜBUNG 4

The first night Timmy did not sleep very well. He didn't have his teddy and it was not quiet enough at the camping site. At home he didn't sleep in the same bed with Kate. She didn't leave him enough room and she didn't want him in "her" bed. So Timmy wasn't warm enough. He didn't have nice dreams and was not happy that night.

ÜBUNG 5

Mögliche Antworten:
Timmy was not sick anymore. He felt better.
Tom didn't do any homework. He wrote a letter to Jenny.
Kate didn't stay in the caravan. She looked for new friends.
Mr Mason didn't lie on the beach. He went for a walk.
Mrs Mason didn't cook in the caravan. She bought a new teddy for Timmy.

ÜBUNG 6

1. Did you ...? Yes, I did.
2. Did you ...? Yes, I did.
3. Did you ...? Yes, I did.
4. Was it ...? No, it wasn't.
5. Did you ...? Yes, I did.
6. Did you ...? Yes, I did.
7. Were there ...? Yes, there were.
8. Did you ...? No, I didn't.
9. Were they ...? No, they weren't.
10. Where they ...? Yes, they were.

ÜBUNG 7

Mögliche Fragen:
- Where is Timmy?
- What happened?
- Is Timmy hurt?
- Did he break anything?
- How did it happen?
- Where did it happen?
- Did anybody help him?
- Did anybody call a doctor?
- How far is it from here?

etc.

ÜBUNG 8

- Did it hurt, Timmy?
- How did the accident happen?
- Why didn't you see the stone?
- Did you fall on your arm?
- Did you cry?
- When did you break your arm?
- Was your teddy all right?
- Who helped you?
- Was anybody with you?

ÜBUNG 9

- He was allowed to play with his teddy.
- He was allowed to draw a picture with his right arm.
- He was allowed to talk to the nurses./He could talk to the nurses.
- He didn't have to make his bed.
- He wasn't allowed to run around in the room.
- He was allowed to look at his picture book.
- He had to be careful with his arm.
- He had to keep his arm still.
- He didn't have to clean the room.
- He wasn't allowed to play in the corridor.
- He didn't have to stay in bed all day.
- He had to eat his meals.

ÜBUNG 10

Mögliche Lösungen:
- Were you allowed to play with your teddy? – Yes, I was.
- Were you allowed to draw pictures with your right arm? – Yes, I was.
- Could you talk to the nurses? – Yes, I could.
- Did you have to make your bed? – No, I didn't.
- Were you allowed to run around in the room? – No, I wasn't.
- Were you allowed to look at your picture book? – Yes, I was.
- Did you have to be careful with your arm? – Yes, I did.
- Did you have to keep your arm still? – Yes, I did.
- Did you have to clean your room? – No, I didn't.
- Were you allowed to play in the corridor? – No, I wasn't.
- Did you have to stay in bed all day? – No, I didn't.
- Did you have to eat your meals? – Yes, I did.

16 Simple past und past progressive im Vergleich

ÜBUNG 1

First Tom sent Kate back to their parents.
So Kate ran back to the caravan.
Then she told her parents all about Timmy's accident.
Then Mrs Mason phoned a doctor.
When the doctor arrived, she examined Timmy.
After that she called an ambulance.
When the ambulance arrived, the ambulance men put Timmy on a stretcher.
After that they drove him to the hospital.

ÜBUNG 2

When Timmy had a accident,
a woman was reading a magazine,
a man was lying in a deckchair,
some people were swimming,
two children were playing with a ball,
a girl was putting on her clothes,
a boy was listening to a radio,
a family was having a picnic

ÜBUNG 3

Mögliche Fragen:
What were you doing when the accident happened?
Were you having a swim?
Were you playing on the beach?
Were you reading a magazine?
etc.
Were you sleeping?
Were you watching the sea/ the boys/the girls?
Were you listening to your radio?

ÜBUNG 4

Mögliche Antworten:
When poor Timmy broke his arm,
– Mr Mason was drinking beer with their neighbours,
– Mr Mason was smoking and talking,
– his wife was lying in the sun,
– she was just having breakfast,
– Kate was just getting up,
– Tom was writing a letter,
– nobody was looking after him.

ÜBUNG **5**

1. While they were sitting in the waiting-room, the door opened. A man came in.
2. He was wearing a bandage round his head.
3. He said good morning. Then he sat down and looked for a newspaper.
4. He opened the newspaper and began to read.
5. While he was reading his newspaper, a nurse came in.
6. She told Mr Mason and Mrs Mason to follow her.
7. She led them to the room where Timmy was waiting.
8. There a doctor was talking to Timmy.
9. Timmy was asking him a lot of questions.
10. When the doctor saw them, he called them to Timmy's bed.
11. Timmy was laughing. He was happy that he could go home.
12. They thanked the doctor and packed Timmy's things. Then they left the hospital.

ÜBUNG **6**

I was playing football when I fell to the ground and broke my arm.
I was climbing a rock when I slipped.
I slipped when I was having a shower. I broke three ribs.
I was cleaning the windows when the ladder broke. I fell onto the floor.
I was lying in my deckchair when it collapsed.
I was doing my homework when I fell asleep. I fell off the chair.

ÜBUNG **7**

Timmy still had to be very careful – he couldn't go for a swim – everybody had to keep him busy – Tom often read ghost stories to him – Timmy's favourite story was about an American family who wanted to buy – When they came to the castle, the sun was not shining – it was raining and thunder sounded again and again – When they entered the castle – a flash of lightning filled – and there was lightning – when they came down – they saw blood – the next night they heard – when Mr Otis opened – he saw – long hair fell from his head – his eyes were like fire ...

17 Simple past und present perfect im Vergleich

ÜBUNG 1

1. When did you come back?
2. Where did you go?
3. Did you like your stay there?
4. Have you ever been to Italy?
5. Did you do anything for school as Old Misery told you?
6. Did you play tennis in the holidays?
7. How many postcards did you write?
8. Where did you buy these shoes?
9. What was the weather like? Did it rain a lot?
10. Have you already seen Mike?

ÜBUNG 2

Mögliche Antworten:
– I came back ...
– I went to ... /I stayed ...
– Yes, I did/No, I didn't.
– Yes, I have/No, I haven't.
– Yes, I did/No, I didn't.
– Yes, I did/No, I didn't.
– I wrote ... postcards/I didn't write any postcards.
– I bought them ...
– It was fine/hot/very warm/lovely. Yes, it did/No, it didn't.
– No, I haven't.

ÜBUNG 3

We stayed there for two weeks.
We always went swimming there.
We had an accident, but we haven't repaired it yet.

We visited the castle. Did you know that Charles was a prisoner there?
I played with him a lot. We often went to the beach and had a swim together.
We played with her sometimes.

ÜBUNG 4

- I haven't been late any more. I was only late the first day.
- I have nearly always listened to my teachers.
- I have never again played during lessons.
- I have only sometimes talked to my neighbour.
- I haven't forgotten my books again. I forgot them only yesterday.
- I have done my homework in all subjects. I only didn't do it last Monday.
- I have usually gone home immediately after school.
- I have written better tests and got good marks.
- I have learned more German. Yesterday I nearly spent ten minutes on my German homework.
- I haven't watched so much TV. Yesterday I only watched one hour.

ÜBUNG 5

- We came back yesterday.
- I often went swimming.
- I got to know a German boy.
- I met Mike in the holidays.
- I talked a lot of German.
- We had an accident.
- I didn't do any homework in the holidays.
- I have become really fat.
- I ate too much in the holidays.
- We visited a lot of castles in the holidays.

ÜBUNG 6

In the holidays we visited Carisbrooke Castle. Carisbrooke Castle is an old castle. It is famous, too, because Charles was a prisoner there ... People say that he hasn't found peace yet and that his ghost is still walking there.
When we got there, the sky was very dark. When we walked through the entrance, it began to rain. So we went into the castle, but it was very dark in there, too. There were lots of strange noises. Suddenly a door opened. When I looked there, I saw something green. It was coming towards me. I ran out of the building and told everything to my parents. They didn't believe me. They just laughed at me.
Two days after the holidays were over we had to go home again. That night I went to bed early, but woke up at midnight. There was a strange noise again. I saw something green. It was sitting at my desk, but before I could say anything, it was gone. I soon forgot this, but two weeks later I woke up again. I saw a green shadow at my desk again. It was writing something in an exercise book. I was very afraid and did not move. Five minutes later it was gone. As it didn't come back, I got up and went to the desk. There I saw my exercise book. It was open, but there was a note in the book: This is what the ghost told me and that's why I did not do any homework last Tuesday.

ÜBUNG 7

Mögliche Antworten:
I couldn't do any homework because
– my neighbour was ill.
– I left my book at school.
– my mother/father/sister was ill yesterday.
– I felt so ill in the afternoon.
– my pen did not work.
– I forgot my schoolbag.
– my exercise book was full.
– I had to repair my bike.
– my mother had no time to do it.

I can't show you my homework because
– I have left it on the bus/at home.
– I have forgotten my schoolbag.
– my baby brother/sister has eaten it.
– my baby brother has made a plane out of it.

18 Adjektive

ÜBUNG 1

Mögliche Antworten:
My friend? He is tall and thin, but he is very strong, too.
My friend? She is fat and small, but she is exciting, too.
My sister? She is nice and funny, but she can be difficult, too.
My brother? He noisy and fat, but he but he can be nice, too.

ÜBUNG 2

Mögliche Antworten:
Comics are boring/interesting/wonderful/exciting/fantastic ...
Films are boring/funny/interesting/exciting/wonderful ...
Books are interesting/exciting/wonderful/fantastic/funny ...
Football is exciting/boring/fantastic/dangerous/interesting/difficult ...
TV is boring/bad/exciting/fantastic/dangerous/interesting ...
English tests are wonderful/fantastic/exciting/funny/interesting ...
Boys are exciting/dangerous/wonderful/clever/intelligent ...
Teachers are loud/boring/dangerous/strange/crazy ...
Baby brothers/sisters are loud/fat/noisy/boring ...
Pop music is beautiful/fantastic/wonderful/loud ...
Girls are noisy/difficult/boring/beautiful ...

ÜBUNG 3

a funny girl	– a boring girl
an old town	– a new/modern town
a small boy	– a tall boy
a good mark	– a bad mark
a boring film	– an exciting/interesting film
a fast runner	– a slow runner
a bad driver	– a good driver
a clever pupil	– a silly pupil
a quiet boy	– a noisy boy
a happy child	– an unhappy child
a difficult text	– an easy text
a silly person	– an intelligent person
a terrible story	– a nice story
a rich man	– a poor man

ÜBUNG 4

good, better, the best; careful, more careful, the most careful; noisy, noisier, the noisiest; fat, fatter, the fattest; powerful, more powerful, the most powerful; nice, nicer, the nicest; intelligent, more intelligent, the most intelligent; heavy, heavier, the heaviest; dangerous, more dangerous, the most dangerous; quick, quicker, the quickest.

ÜBUNG 5

Mögliche Antworten:
Tom's dad is the tallest in the family. He is taller than Grandpa and he is taller than his wife. Tom is the tallest of the children. Kate and Timmy are smaller than Tom. Timmy is the smallest of them all.

ÜBUNG 6

Susan: I think tennis is more difficult than swimming.
Betty: No, it isn't, but it's more expensive.
Susan: More expensive? I think swimming is as expensive as tennis.

Susan: I think English is nicer than German.
Betty: No, it isn't, but it's more useful.
Susan: More useful? I think it's as useful as English.

Susan: I think comics are funnier than books.
Betty: No, they aren't, but books are more interesting than comics.
Susan: More interesting? I think comics are as interesting as books.

ÜBUNG 7

Susan:
I think he's the tallest boy in our class.
He must be the strongest boy ...
It has got the same colour as your hair.
I need somebody who is cleverer than Tom. You know, at maths Tom is even worse than me.
Anne told me his photos are the best photos she has ever seen.

Jane:
No, I think David is taller than him.
He is even nicer than Tom.
... or you'll get a prize for the silliest question.
He looks a bit silly, but perhaps he is better at maths than he looks.

ÜBUNG 8

1. Has your English become better?
2. Let's hope it hasn't become worse.
3. Is the number of mistakes in your English tests smaller or bigger now?
4. Were the exercises very boring?
5. Were they more interesting than in your textbook?
6. Were they as boring as in your textbook?
7. Or were they worse?
8. Was the grammar clear enough?
9. Or was the grammar in your textbook easier?
10. We hope that you didn't find things too difficult.

19 Adverbien

ÜBUNG 1

1. She dances well.
2. He runs fast.
3. She sings beautifully.
4. She does everything quietly.
5. He always runs araund noisily.
6. She works hard.
7. She always answers cleverly.
8. He always laughs happily.
9. She dances terribly.
10. He speaks German very well.

ÜBUNG 2

Mögliche Lösungen:

a) I can speak English very well. I also play football very well. I am a good worker and do my homework very carefully. My teachers think that I'm very intelligent. I always answer cleverly and do things intelligently. I understand things easily, too. etc.

b) My friend is a bit slow. He does everything very slowly, but he does things carefully. He doesn't speak English very well, but he is very good at maths. He only writes very badly, so I can't read it very easily. Sometimes he is a bit boring, but he sings wonderfully. etc.

ÜBUNG 3

All the children were quietly sitting ... Could it be one of those silly fire alarms? ... Smoke was coming out in thick clouds ... and in one room they saw red flames. They were all very excited... "Be quiet and sit all down", the teacher shouted angrily. "You needn't be afraid. You Pete, get up quickly. ... don't run: let's leave it slowly and in good order. Keep together and remember to shut the door carefully. Leave your things in the room if you can't pack them quickly. Are you all ready? Let's get out slowly now; ... be sure to shut the door behind you."

ÜBUNG 4

1. Lots of windows were still open.
2. Some pupils were running around excitedly.
3. Others were still quietly packing their things.
4. One pupil was busily copying his homework ... He wasn't even writing very fast.
5. He didn't think it was dangerous to remain in the building.
6. Some were excitedly watching the smoke ...
7. Others were happy that there was a fire at their school.
8. A good fire is less boring than an English lesson, one of them said excitedly.
9. And there will be no English tomorrow, somebody else added quickly.

ÜBUNG 5

Mögliche Lösungen:

- Leave your things in the classroom; get out of that room quickly.
- Shut the windows/the door carefully.
- Where is the register? Look for it immediately.
- Get up quickly. Don't be so slow.
- Shut the door immediately. Get out of the building immediately.
- Don't be excited. Don't be so noisy. Don't talk so loud. Leave the room quietly.
- Aren't you good runners? Run as fast as you can.

etc.

ÜBUNG 6

1. Get out of the way, one man shouted angrily.
2. Four men jumped out of it quickly.
3. Two of them ran into the building quickly.
4. They busily raised a ladder (busily).
5. One man (carefully) climbed up the ladder carefully.
6. Another man quickly fetched the water hose (quickly).
7. "Is there anybody injured?", another man asked worriedly.
8. "Where can we take the water from?", one man asked nervously.
9. "What are we waiting for?", another man shouted angrily.
10. "Where do we begin?", one man asked excitedly.

20 Die Wortstellung im Englischen

ÜBUNG 1

Mögliche Antworten:
Before I go to school, I usually do my homework.
When I don't want to go to school, I tell my mum that I am ill.
When it's too cold to get up, I stay in bed.
When I am late, I don't have breakfast.
When I must go to bed, I still read an hour or two.
Before I get up, I often think that it is too early to get up.
Before I have breakfast, I usually wash.
When I go to bed, I switch off the lights.
When I can't find my homework, I get angry.

ÜBUNG 2

On Monday, I am going to play table tennis with Tom at 4 p.m.
On Tuesday, I am going to watch a film on TV at 8.15.
On Wednesday, I am going to learn for a German test with Tom.
On Thursday, I am going to help Kate with her maths homework.
On Friday, I am going to buy a birthday present for Sarah; then I am going to ring her up.
On Saturday, I am going to go to Sarah's birthday party.
On Sunday, I am going to ring up Tom and go for a walk with him ...

ÜBUNG 3

On Monday, I am going to play football.
On Tuesday, I am going to ...
On Wednesday, ...
etc.

ÜBUNG **4**

1. Today I am ill.
2. Today I needn't get up.
3. Today I can stay in bed.
4. Today I needn't go to school.
5. Today I needn't do any homework.
6. Today I have got no German.
7. Today I have got a temperature.
8. Today is a beautiful day.

ÜBUNG **5**

Sarah:
Brr ... Pudding again. I really don't like pudding.

Christine:
Ugh ... Sausages. I had them yesterday. I can't eat sausages every day.

Joe:
... I had an egg this morning. I don't want another egg now.

Tom:
I like chocolate pudding. If you don't want your chocolate pudding, you can give it to me.

Sandra to Kevin:
... I could eat chips from morning to night.

Kevin:
... I think I'll have it. Do you take fruit salad, too, Sandra?

ÜBUNG **6**

1. English pupils already go to school when they are five.
2. Most British pupils go to a comprehensive school when they are eleven.
3. They can leave school when they are 16.
4. In many schools they must wear school uniform.
5. The school colours in Tom's school are blue and grey.
6. The pupils' parents can buy the school uniforms in special shops.
7. In most English schools lessons begin later than in Germany.
8. Most English pupils also have lessons in the afternoon.
9. There are lessons in the afternoon, so many English schools have school cafeterias.
10. Pupils can have lunch at the school cafetiera during break.
11. In many English schools pupils learn to cook.

ÜBUNG 7

Fragen:
– What subjects do you have on Monday?
– What do you have in the first lesson?
– What do you do in the break?
– When and where do you see Jenny?
– Do you have lunch in the school cafeteria?
– When do you do your homework?
– Where do you do your homework?

Mögliche Antworten:
– On Monday, I have got maths, biology, geography, English and German.
– In the first two lessons I have got maths. In the third and fourth lesson I have got biology. In the afternoon I first have geography, then English. My last lesson on Monday is German.
– In the break I talk to Jenny/I play with Mike ...
– I see Jenny every morning and every afternoon. She is in my class!
– Usually I have lunch at home, but sometimes I have lunch in the school cafeteria, too.
– I usually do my homework when I come home from school.
– I usually do it in my room.

ÜBUNG 8

There are pupils
– who usually forget their homework.
– who have never forgotten their homework.
– who often do their homework at school.
– who have never copied it from their neighbours.
– who never know what they must do.
– who never write down what they must do.
– who always forget their homework at home.
– who usually do it on the way to school.
– who sometimes leave their exercise book at home.
– who sometimes forget it on the bus.

ÜBUNG 9

Mögliche Antworten:

1. I usually do my homework./Yes, I do.
2. I usually/always do it in the afternoon/in the evening/in the morning.
3. I usually do it at home/on the bus/at school.
4. I don't usually forget it./No, I don't.
5. I sometimes forget it when I have got no time/when I don't think of it.
6. I never copy it from my neighbour./No, never. I only sometimes copy it from him.
7. No, I'm not. I usually play with my neighbour or talk to him.
8. No, they don't. They don't often help me/Yes, they do. They often help me.
9. He often helps me in ...
10. Yes, he has/No, he hasn't. He has never helped me.

1 Wörter mit „o"/„oo"

ÜBUNG 1

It's a shoe.
It's a boot.
It's not new, it's old.
One and one is two.
They're brother and sister.
It's a book.

s	h	o	e			
b	o	o	t			
o	l	d				
t	w	o				
b	r	o	t	h	e	r
b	o	o	k			

ÜBUNG 2

a) ~~God~~ Good morning, John.

b) Tom: "Is the cat in the ~~hause~~ house?"

c) Tom's ~~mather~~ mother is at home.

ÜBUNG 3

1. They're in the school-bag.
2. It's a shoe.
3. She's two.
4. It's on the floor.
5. No, he's in the house.
6. No, she's at school.

2 Die Zahlen bis 100 – Die Uhrzeit

ÜBUNG 1

		o	n	e
t	w	o		
	f	o	u	r

		t	h	r	e	e	
t	h	i	r	t	e	e	n
	f	i	f	t	e	e	n

		f	i	v	e
		s	e	v	e	n
	e	l	e	v	e	n
t	w	e	l	v	e	

ÜBUNG 2

late – eight
too – two
pen – ten
key – three
floor – four
(to) drive – five
(to) shine – nine
(He) picks – six

ÜBUNG 3

a) telephone – one
b) three – tree
c) seven oder eleven
d) two – who
e) four – hour
f) four – your
g) one – on
h) nine – in
i) two – to

ÜBUNG 4

a) fifteen
b) eighteen

ÜBUNG 5

two – twenty
three – thirty
four – forty (!)
five – fifty (!)
six – sixty
seven – seventy
eight – eighty
nine – ninety
ten – a hundred!

ÜBUNG 6

a) five – fifteen – fifty, four – fourteen – forty
b) forty-four, fifty-five
c) one hundred

ÜBUNG 7

£ six hundred and fifty
$ five hundred and seventy-five

ÜBUNG 8

a) It's seven o'clock.
b) A minute has 60 seconds.
c) It's five minutes to nine.
d) It's half past nine.
e) It's a quarter to ten.

ÜBUNG **9**

It's two to two. (13.58)

ÜBUNG **10**

a) It's a quarter to eleven.

b) You must wait half an hour.

3 Wörter mit „o"/„oo"/„ou"

ÜBUNG **1**

langes „u" [u:]: boot, school, two, who, afternoon, shoe, too

kurzes „u" [u]: good, book, look

ÜBUNG **2**

a) your b) now c) woman d) home e) four

ÜBUNG **3**

[əu]: biro window [u]: foot woman [u:]: too two

ÜBUNG **4**

L	O	O	K					
D	O	O	R					
W	I	N	D	O	W			
G	O	O	D					
P	I	S	T	O	L			
A	F	T	E	R	N	O	O	N

['lʌndən]

ÜBUNG **5**

"Have you got one or two brothers?" – "I've got two brothers."
"Have you got a sister, too?" – "No, I haven't."

ÜBUNG **6**

… "Oh, crocodiles, too? How many?" – "Two or three I think." …

4 Farben – Kleidungsstücke

ÜBUNG 1

	b	l	u	e				
		g	r	e	y			
w	h	i	t	e				
		g	r	e	e	n		
			r	e	d			
			y	e	l	l	o	w

ÜBUNG 2

a) brown b) pink c) black

ÜBUNG 3

a) yellow; black and white; grey; white

b) He is pink before and blue after.

ÜBUNG 4

blouse – tights – raincoat Kevin's shirt; Kate's skirt

ÜBUNG 5

a pair of sandals, jeans, socks, wellies, stockings, tights, shorts

ÜBUNG 6

The boy's trousers and tie are too short.
His shoes are too big.

The girl's blazer and skirt are too long.
Her sunhat is too small.

5 Besondere Schreibweisen

ÜBUNG 1

a) The weather is wonderful today.

b) Kevin always goes to school by bus.

c) A washing-machine is very useful.

d) In this shop you can buy almost everything.

e) Mr Bennett is a careful driver.

f) It's seven o'clock and Molly is already in bed.

g) Does your friend also play table tennis?

ÜBUNG 2

a) Where's the end of the street?

b) It's warm today, you can take your pullover off.

c) You must get off at the next bus stop.

d) Mr Johnson's shop is on the corner of the street.

e) What's the name of this town?

f) When Molly's cat sees the neighbour's dog, she always runs off.

ÜBUNG 3

a) What colour (a) is the children's rabbit?

b) Tom and Betty laugh (u) at Molly's dirty cat.

c) The boy is too fat, he can't climb through (t) the small window.

d) Our neighbour (u) is a very friendly man.

e) The Parkers have eggs and sausages (m) for breakfast.

f) Scotland is a beautiful (n) country.

Die überflüssigen Buchstaben bilden das Wort autumn.

6 Groß- und Kleinschreibung

ÜBUNG 1

a) Edinburgh is the capital of Scotland

b) The shortest month in the year is February.

c) You get presents from your relatives and friends on your birthday.

d) We give each other presents at Christmas.

e) Your mother's father is your grandfather.

f) The coldest time of the year is winter.

g) My mother's brother is my uncle.

h) The Rolls Royce is an English car.

i) In France the people speak French.

j) Every Sunday many people go to church.

ÜBUNG 2

a) Big fire at supermarket in Oxford Street

b) No trains to South Wales today

c) Coldest Christmas since winter of 1989

d) More German sports cars on Britain's roads

e) Fewer jobs in the south of England

f) Baby Tina's dad is 84!

g) Many more fish in the River Thames

ÜBUNG 3

High Street, England BN1 4PE, Wednesday 3rd May, Dear Uncle Alex, This, letter, I, you, spring, Easter, Germany, Love

ÜBUNG 4

a) My birthday party is on Friday April 8th/8th April/April 8/8 April. …

b) My birthday party is on Sunday July 17th/17th July/July 17/17 July. …

c) … It's on Saturday October 12th/12th October/October12/12 October.

d) My birthday party is on Wednesday February 28th/28th February/ February 28/28 February.

7 Falsche Freunde

ÜBUNG 1

January	February	March	April	May	June
July	August	September	October	November	December

ÜBUNG 2

a) doctor
b) correct
c) perfect
d) theatre
e) music
f) subject
g) exact
h) British
i) physics
j) Scottish
k) fish
l) picnic

ÜBUNG 3

Ein Tick anders!

a) banana
b) marmalade
c) swam
d) glass
e) tea
f) assistant
g) coffee
h) magazine
i) hundred
j) medicine
k) before
l) summer
m) family
n) postcard
o) group
p) soup
q) chocolate
r) tomato

8 Gleich und ähnlich klingende Wörter

ÜBUNG 1

a) red – read
b) blew – blue
c) through – threw
d) new – knew
e) road – rode
f) wood – would
g) break – brake
h) here – hear
i) I – eye
j) knows – nose
k) two – to/too
l) weak – week
m) eight – ate
n) wear – where
o) meat – meet
p) their – there

ÜBUNG 2

a) We had a barbecue *(Grillfest)* last week. I ate <u>eight</u> sausages!

b) You're too big for <u>your</u> jeans.

c) Bye-bye! I'm going shopping now. I want to <u>buy</u> some food.

d) <u>Would</u> you like to go for a walk in the wood?

e) Our train leaves in an <u>hour</u>.

f) <u>Who's</u> the boy whose dictations are always full of mistakes?

g) She <u>knows</u> that her nose is a bit too long.

h) Two pounds is <u>too</u> much <u>to</u> pay for a hamburger!

i) <u>Write</u> these words on the right side of your vocabulary notebook.

j) Of course we <u>knew</u> about that new café in the High Street.

k) I've got something in my <u>eye</u>.

l) <u>Their</u> bikes are lying on the grass over there.

m) Can you <u>hear</u> me? – No. Where are you? – Over here!

ÜBUNG 3

1 B					
2 R	E	3 A	D		
O		T			4 B
5 K	N	E	6 W		L
E			O		E
	7 T	H	R	E	W
			E		

ÜBUNG **4**

a) Yesterday we went for a walk in the country.

b) It was very quiet there,

c) and the air was much cleaner than in the town!

d) We had a picnic in the woods and then we went home.

e) On the way home my sister fell and hurt her foot.

f) We had to carry her to the bus stop! When we got home, my feet hurt, too!

g) But we had a wonderful day. Do you want to come with us next time?

h) "Don't forget to feed your hamster!" –

i) "I gave him some food this morning.

j) He looks quite happy." –

k) "He won't live very long if you don't give him enough to eat !"

l) My parents have good jobs. They work in an office in London.

9 „Silent letters" – Buchstaben, die nicht ausgesprochen werden

ÜBUNG **1**

		1 K	N	2 O	W		3 C	U	4 T	
		N		N					I	
5 W	R	I	T	E	6 R		7 H	I	G	H
R		F			I				H	
8 O	N	E	9 S		10 G	H	O	S	T	
N			E		H				11 S	12 O
G		13 C	A	S	T	L	E			N

ÜBUNG **2**

a) Kreide chalk

b) arm poor

c) Wann? When?

d) Fluss river

e) Auto car

f) früh early

g) zuhören listen

h) Gabel fork

i) Wer? Who?

j) brachte brought

ÜBUNG 3

Guess, where, friend, Northern, Germany, her, live, island, near, first, foreign, suitcase, guitar, hours, thirsty, when, biscuits, fruit, juice, friend, her, were, under, sign, Their, house, building, above

"New" silent letters:

-g-	-i-	-u-	-s-	h- (am Wortanfang)	-e (am Wortende)
foreign	friend	guess	island	hours	where
sign	suitcase	guitar			live
	fruit	biscuits			suitcase
	juice	building			juice
					were
					house
					above

ÜBUNG 4

a) Can you guess where my Aunt Rosemary lives?

b) In an old castle! She works there.

c) Don't laugh! It isn't a joke and she isn't a ghost!

d) She is a guide.

e) She lives in a modern flat in one of the old buildings.

f) The castle is on a small island in the middle of a lake.

g) Visitors come by boat through a gate in the high wall.

h) My aunt locks the gate and switches off the lights every night.

i) But she is safe enough. No one could climb the walls!

j) I know you are interested in old buildings.

k) Would you like to visit this castle? Should we go there next week?

10 Laute und ihre Schreibweisen (I)

ÜBUNG 1

a) My little brother loves toast with butter and honey.

b) Does your mother give you enough pocket money *(Taschengeld)*?

c) Mrs Brown's young son is sitting in the sun.

d) My mum doesn't want to come to the football match.

e) Last month I won £100 in the National Lottery.

f) Schreibweise „u": butter, sun, mum

g) Schreibweise „o": brother, loves, honey, mother, money, son, come, month, won

h) Schreibweise „ou": enough, young

i) Schreibweise „oe": does, doesn't

ÜBUNG 2

			1 W		2 S	
		3 W	O	R	K	
	4 F		R		I	
5 B	I	R	D		R	
	R				T	
	6 S	U	R	F		
	T			7 H	E	R

ÜBUNG 3

[ʌ] wie in *but*	[ɜː] wie in *her*
cup	nervous
cousin	sir
double	term
hungry	perfect
trouble	purse
	verb
	thirsty

11 Die Kurzformen der Hilfsverben

ÜBUNG 1

a) "I'm learning English at school."

b) "We've got a good teacher."

c) "She's English but her husband's German."

d) "They've got two daughters, Penny and Tanya."

e) "They haven't got a son".

f) "Penny's in my class at school."

g) "She isn't very good at English."

h) "But her mother's a very good teacher."

i) "What's your English teacher like?"

ÜBUNG 2

a) "My mother has got a good job.

b) She is a truck-driver!

c) Do not laugh! It is true!

d) My father has got a small haulage company.

e) My dad is always very busy.

f) He can not do all the work himself.

g) Mum's job is very interesting.

h) It will not be easy for her to do all the housework without help."

ÜBUNG 3

a) "What are you doing this afternoon?" – "We're going swimming.

b) Do you want to come with us?" – "No, I won't have time.

c) Where were you yesterday?" – "We were at school."

d) "Is Jennifer in your class at school?" – "Who's Jennifer?"

e) "My best friend. Don't you know her?" – "Is she the girl whose brother works at the garage?"

f) "I think so. But he's much older than his sister.

g) They live in your street." – "Oh, I know! Their house is on the corner."

h) "That's right. It's a big house with its own swimming pool in the garden! They're a rich family.

i) I'm going to visit her tomorrow. Can you come, too?" – "Sorry, I want to go shopping after school tomorrow."

j) "Well, I hope you're not too busy to come to my birthday party next week!"

k) "Is it your birthday next week? A party? I'd love to come!"

12 Laute und ihre Schreibweisen (II)

ÜBUNG 1

a) It is often very hot in Australia.

b) You've got a lot of CDs. I want to see them.

c) I bought these sausages at the butcher's shop.

d) What's wrong? – I forgot to put on my watch this morning!

e) Alois is from Innsbruck. He's an Austrian.

f) Schreibweise „o“: hot, got, lot, shop, wrong, forgot, on, from

g) Schreibweise „a“: want, What, watch

h) Schreibweise „au“: Australia, sausages, Austrian

ÜBUNG 2

a) far – ~~cat~~ – postcard – ~~Carol~~ – park – dark

b) hard – ~~happy~~ – ~~caravan~~ – ~~daughter~~ – half – laugh

c) aunt – ~~Australia~~ – laugh – ~~caught~~ – part – heart

ÜBUNG 3

[ɔ:]: port, door, saw, bought, fourteen, warm, hall, water, daughter, thought, wall

= insgesamt 11 Wörter, die den Vokal [ɔ:] enthalten

ÜBUNG 4

[ɑ:] wie in „car“	[ɔ:] wie in „for“	[ɒ] wie in „hot“
hard	sport	forest
class	fault	what
pass	warm	shock
bar	ball	
	strawberry	
	fork	

13 Zusammensetzungen: Bindestrich? Zwei Worte? Ein Wort?

ÜBUNG 1

a) Number twenty-four came thirtieth.

b) Number forty-seven came thirty-first.

c) Number ninety-nine came thirty-second.

d) Number fifty-three came thirty-third.

e) Number sixty-one came thirty-fourth.

f) Number eighty-five came thirty-fifth.

ÜBUNG 2

a) "Listen! I think I can hear somebody upstairs in the bedroom."

b) "But there's nobody else in the house. We're alone.

c) I can't hear anything."

d) "I sometimes hear things at night, too."

e) "Don't worry. There's nothing to worry about. I'm here with you."

f) "I'm hungry. Have we got anything to eat?"

g) "There are some things in the fridge. Let's have a look. Are you thirsty?"

h) "No. I've already had three glasses of Coke."

i) "Look. Mum has made us some sandwiches. They're all ready to eat."

j) "That's all right, then! Let's eat!

k) Mum and Dad will be back at ten o' clock anyway."

Merkzettel

Diese „Wortpaare" schreibe ich zusammen:	Diese „Wortpaare" schreibe ich getrennt:
somebody	some things
nobody	all ready
anything	all right
sometimes	
nothing	
already	
anyway	

14 Laute und ihre Schreibweisen (III)

ÜBUNG 1

		[ʊ] wie in „pull"	[ʌ] wie „but"
a) *Mother:*	Just look at your room, Jason!	look	Just
b)	Pick up your books and	books	up
c)	put them in your cupboard!	put	cupboard
d) *Jason:*	But it's already full, Mum!	full	But, Mum
e) *Mother:*	Well, would you put them under your bed, please?	would, put	under

ÜBUNG 2

a) I'm looking for a book about Indian cooking.

b) Who's that woman over there? –

c) I can see three women. Do you mean the one in the orange dress?

d) Shut the door and sit down on the floor.

e) He is more interested in his hobbies than in his school work.

f) Do you like French, too?

g) The opposite of "rich" is "poor".

h) The food is very good.

Schreibweise „oo"			Schreibweise „o"		
[ʊ] wie „look" (kurz)	[uː] wie „too" (lang)	[ɔː] wie „or" (lang)	[ɒ] wie „of" (kurz)	[uː] wie „too" (lang)	[ɔː] wie „or" (lang)
looking book cooking good	school too food	door floor	orange hobbies opposite	Who Do Do	more

Welche Wörter konntest du *nicht* einordnen? Es sind die Wörter: woman und women. Merke dir die Schreibweise dieser Wörter besonders gut!

ÜBUNG **3**

a) He asked me to meet him at three o'clock.

b) We can have a cup of tea or coffee on the beach.

c) PLEASE DO NOT PUT YOUR FEET ON THE SEATS

d) I had a piece of cake after my meal.

e) Too many sweets are bad for your teeth.

f) Our English teacher lives in our street.

g) The police were here last week.

h) She doesn't eat meat or cheese.

i) We needn't wait for the other people.

j) He picked up the telephone receiver and rang his niece up.

k) Please complete these sentences.

ÜBUNG **4**

a) breakfast b) head c) heavy d) ready

ÜBUNG **5**

a) Can you see Kate? b) Yes, she's swimming in the sea.

c) The sea must be cold today, you can see that Kate's skin is blue.

ÜBUNG **6**

a) My father has a new car.

b) I like skiing.

c) We sat down on the floor.

d) We went to the cinema yesterday.

e) The children are lying on the beach.

f) Open the door, please.

ÜBUNG **7**

Unregelmässige Mehrzahlformen

			1 F		2 M			3 C			4 W
		5 W	O	M	A	N		H			O
	6 M		O		N			I			M
7 F	E	E	T					L			E
	N			8 C	H	I	L	D	R	E	N